THE ANGEL IN THE MARBLE

How I chiseled myself free from life in a cult.

BY

MEGAN BINGMAN

Dedication

For my friend Molly, who believed I could do this, and supported my dream to make it happen.

For my husband Jimmy, who gave me the time and opportunity to be a writer.

For my girls, who remind me every day what it means to love someone unconditionally.

This book is a telling of my life story as I remember it. It is told from my perspective. Some names and attributes have been changed to protect the people who may not agree with my recollection, and to protect patient privacy. Any dialogue included may not be exact. I can promise that every detail comes from the heart, and is a statement of my own truth. It may not reflect the truth of others.

The following names have been changed: Kyle, Gabriella, Steven, Jacob, Paul, Brad, Casey, Sarah, June, Kate and Georgia.

"I saw the angel in the marble, and carved until I set him free."

- Michaelangelo

Michaelangelo said that he saw the angel inside of the marble before he even began to sculpt it. He chiseled away at the marble, until he set it free. I would say the same of myself. The marble was Jehovah's Witnesses, the religious cult I was raised in, and I was frozen inside of it. On some intuitive level, I knew I wasn't my true self within the confines of that religion. I saw who I was supposed to be, and I chiseled away at the confines of the cult until I freed myself. I am the angel in the marble. This book is not only the story of how I set myself free, but also how my life was forever changed by the experience of being trapped in that marble in the first place.

TABLE OF CONTENTS

CHAPTER 1

E veryone encounters some level of trauma in their lives. I believe that it is the reason we signed up for this earthly adventure at all. I picture life as a training ground where souls come to learn the lessons that will help them ascend to higher levels of consciousness. "By iron, iron itself is sharpened," right? We become our best selves, we reach our greatest potential, only after we have been sharpened and defined by the traumas that create us show us who we really are. While I am not against any religion in particular, religious trauma has a very special flavor to it. It's not just Jehovah's Witnesses who have the market cornered on religious trauma, and it's not even just religious cults that can instill the deep roots of trauma within a person. What I am trying to bring awareness to by writing this memoir,, is the fact that religion itself can cause trauma that affects us on a cellular level.

Most Christian religions teach that we are born sinners in need of redemption, right? Personally, I take a hard pass on this philosophy. The Bible itself says that God is Love, and that we are made in his image. How can I be anything less than beautiful and worthy if I am made in the image of love? This belief that we are inherently "enough" is not a common one among religious people, and it has taken me years and years of therapy and research to come to accept the idea of God as the vibration of love. During a Kundalini yoga class, I saw the anagram LIGHT in my head. The letters were spelled vertically and from each main letter came another word... Love Is God's Highest Trait. This has become my motto, and frankly, it's the religion I live by. But it wasn't always this way.

I was raised in a dysfunctional home. I've been around long enough and worked with enough people in my role as a healer to know that everyone's home has some level of dysfunction. But I measure my childhood in how its trauma affected me as an adult, and I would say that was significant. We were part of the Jehovah's Witness organization which I realized, later in life, is a religious cult. This was one part of the dysfunction, but certainly not all of it. From the outside looking in, our family had it all together. We were a prime example of what a spiritual family in the "one true religion" should look like. My father was the head elder in our congregation, and my mother was a full time volunteer teaching bible lessons, mostly to the underprivileged in our community. To other people in the congregation, and to the outside world, my parents were shiny, bright, and good. But behind closed doors, our family was the definition of dysfunctional. At home, the tension that filled the air and settled around us like fog in a valley was unbearable. My mother was deeply unhappy, and my father was oblivious to her unhappiness. My sister had severe Social Phobia Disorder. She was unable to speak to a stranger, and struggled to perform activities of daily living like filling her car with gas or ordering a cup of coffee if it involved talking to someone she didn't know. She was also a genius. It wasn't

2

until her early forties that she would be diagnosed with Autistic Spectrum Disorder. At the time, we didn't know anything about her disability. But for as long as I can remember, I felt that it was my responsibility to be her voice in public. Even as her younger sister, for better or for worse, I became her spokesperson.

My father was also extremely smart, and he would often respond to questions or conversations he didn't want to be a part of with a silent stare. I distinctly remember the feeling of being invisible, and therefore worthless, when I would approach my Dad with a question or problem, and he would just stare silently in response and then turn back to his computer. My mother would often complain that she had to ask him "twenty questions" to get any information out of him. Growing up, I assumed this was just how men communicate, but now, looking back, I would bet the farm that my father is also on the Autistic Spectrum.

Many children who grow up in traumatic households learn to be hyper vigilant. We learn that we need to be on our toes twenty-four hours a day, seven days a week, in order to prevent catastrophes. This level of constant vigilance is extremely hard on a developing child. I learned that my role in the family was to be the mediator, the comedian, and the perfect child. I had to be perfect, because my job was to make sure my mom didn't get mad. She would often reach the height of frustration and lose her temper trying to communicate with my sister and my father.

Where my sister and Dad had very limited emotional capacity, I seemed to have the opposite problem. I felt every emotion, whether it was mine, or someone else's, to the core of my being. My emotions felt too big. My feelings felt too dramatic. I was always very aware of what was going on around me, in order to constantly find ways to cut the tension. It was like waves that would build, smaller at first, and then one on top of the other, until our home felt about as safe as a tsunami. I would do anything to avoid feeling these overwhelming emotions, so my constant goal was to alleviate the pressure. When my mother would lose her temper and scream, I felt a level of fear that should only be experienced in life threatening situations. My body always over-reacted. I felt her frustration within the deepest part of my body, and I felt like it was always my fault for not easing her pain. I walked around with my chest and stomach tight with fear. Yet, at meetings, or spiritual gatherings, I turned on the charm, threw my shoulders back, and acted as if I was happy and healthy. I was a goddamn beacon of Jehovah's light on earth. As a coping mechanism, I learned how to split myself in pieces. I knew that I needed to be one way in public, a way that would "honor the name of God" since I proudly called myself one of his "witnesses." I also learned that being my true self was not an option.

In public, I was a spiritual child of God, but also the physical child of the head elder. I had to set a standard for how his followers would act. When I was eight or nine, I was doodling in a notebook during one of our two-hour sermons, and a sister–everyone in the congregation is your spiritual sister and brother, and so they are referred to as Sister or Brother (insert last name)--behind me leaned forward and whispered that I needed to stop doodling and pay attention, because it was my responsibility to be an example for the younger children in the congregation. I had been drawing an ice cream cone. I was a child, daydreaming about dessert, and being chastised for not meditating hard enough on spiritual instruction.

In private, I had to develop the skill of learning to read the room very quickly, so that I could intervene when things were about to get ugly. This skill of extreme people pleasing served me very well, not only as a child, but also as I went on to be a wife, parent, foster parent and Myofascial Release Therapist. This ability to say, be, and do whatever people needed from me served me so well that my choice to bury my authentic self became deeply ingrained. I grew up with that core of dysfunction eating me up from the inside like a cancer. This 'gift' of being able to read and respond to what people needed continued through most of my life. People loved the act I could put on, but very few people really knew the actress behind the facade. The belief that making people happy was my responsibility was validated again and again. It was reinforced every time I would play the role they wanted, and they would tell me that I was amazing, good, kind, and a healer. My appointment book was always filled weeks out because patients responded to my ability to really "see" them, support them, and accept them for their true selves. At the same time, deep inside, I was just a broken child begging to be loved and seen for my own true self that I was terrified to show everyone. I knew, at the core of my being, that I was worthless and unlovable. My parents, the cult, and my own broken heart reinforced that belief time after time.

CHAPTER 2

Our religion was not too much different than other Christian religions. We would read and study the New World Translation of the Bible. This Bible was very comparable to the King James Version except that it was written in modern day English and the name Jehovah hadn't been removed from the text. But, if someone asked us to use a different translation, our scriptures matched up pretty well. Reading and knowing our bibles was so important that there was a bible reading schedule that we were all instructed to follow. This schedule would result in each member reading the Bible from cover to cover every three years. We would hold "meetings" three times per week where we would discuss the scriptures, and how to apply them in our lives. These meetings were sometimes smaller in size, and held in people's living rooms, or they would be held in the Kingdom Hall, which was our version of a church. The meetings at the Kingdom Hall would be attended by the entire congregation which was usually eighty to one hundred people. In theory, each of these meetings would help us to understand the scriptures and follow the example of Christ, while bringing the Word of God to our neighbors, whether they liked it or not.

Although Jehovah's Witnesses could accurately be classed as a Christian religion, there were definitely things that made us stand out from other religions. Most notably, Jehovah's Witnesses do not celebrate holidays, except for the Memorial of Christ's death which is a rather somber occasion held around Easter each year. At the Memorial, Jehovah's Witnesses around the world would all gather on the same night to commemorate that Jesus gave his life for our sins. We would honor his sacrifice by passing around a tray of unleavened bread and a glass of wine. Usually, my mother would obtain the body and blood of Jesus at the grocery store the day of the service. Only those who were part of the 144,000 anointed ones would partake of the bread and wine. Witnesses believe that only 144,000 people would be anointed to rule with Jesus in heaven. They would rule with Jesus over the rest of his faithful witnesses, who would get to live forever on a paradise earth with their resurrected loved ones. Apparently there was a super secret way to tell if you were part of this anointed group of witnesses that got to partake. In our congregation, there was only one proclaimed anointed brother. He was disfellowshipped, or shunned, from the congregation for having premarital sex, but he continued to show up each year and partake, which infuriated my mother. I believe she bought the cheapest blood of Jesus, and the stalest body of Christ she could buy each year for him to consume, out of pure righteous indignation. Aside from this ceremony, the Witnesses abstain from celebrating all other holidays.

Jehovah's Witnesses are probably the most well known for not celebrating birthdays. Their reasoning is that there were only two birthdays in the Bible, and on both of those occasions a true believer of Jehovah was murdered. They believe that since birthdays were only portrayed in the Bible in that negative light, it is a sign that true Christians should not celebrate them. They also feel that celebrating birthdays glorifies the person being celebrated, and we should only give our glory to God. So, as a child I grew up with zero acknowledgment of my own birthday. My very first memory is of running around the dining room, bouncing off of the dining room chairs as my mother dusted in preparation for our small group bible study at the house. I was joyously singing "I'm three today! I'm three today!" As I bounced between chairs. My mother slammed down her can of pledge and through gritted teeth said "We do NOT celebrate birthdays in this house!" I remember a desperate desire to make myself small in that moment. I had made a mistake. I had done something wrong, and I had disappointed not only my parents, but also Jehovah God. Those unintentional mistakes always felt like a shot to the heart. I hadn't meant to, but my core must be evil, because subconsciously, I wanted to celebrate the day I was born. I also remember thinking that the day I was born didn't matter, and if that was true, I must not matter either. I secretly reveled in the one birthday tradition I still had. My mother's parents, who were never Jehovah's Witnesses, and who were also both music teachers, would call on my birthday and sing "Happy Mmmm Mmmm to you!" I had to act like I was completely offended when I told my parents what they had done, but my mother used to chuckle which made me feel like I wasn't THAT evil for enjoying the tradition.

At school, I would dread someone in my class having a birthday and bringing in birthday treats for us to share. For me to partake in this celebration would be a slap in the face of Jehovah God. It was my duty as one of his true followers to remove myself from this demonic situation, so I had to go to the library and sit by myself until all of the fun was over. I would sit alone in the library, or in the hallway, until the cupcakes had been passed out, and the singing was done. One day, one of the girls I really liked was having her birthday celebration, and she had brought in these really awesome looking smiley face cookies. I wanted to stay for that party more than anything. My teacher told me that it was time to head to the library and I started to cry. The teacher said I could stay, and she wouldn't tell my parents, so I did. I got to be part of the party, and eat that glorious yellow smiley-face cookie, and it was just so wonderful to be included. I didn't sing, because I couldn't justify that level of blasphemy, but just to be a part of the celebration felt so wonderful.

I was riding my high of being included until another girl in class noticed that I had stayed for the party and said "Hey, you didn't eat my cupcake, because you said you're not allowed to celebrate. You are a LIAR because you are here eating Lisa's cookie!" I didn't know how to respond because she was right. I HAD changed my tune. I had been tempted by Satan and proved lacking in faith. The Devil had used that smiley face cookie to see how much I really loved Jehovah God, and I had failed the test. Despite my good intentions, and my overwhelming desire to belong, I had let Jehovah down, and this anger from my fellow classmate was my punishment. When I got home from school, the guilt was all encompassing. I told my mom that I had been weak, and that I ate the birthday cookie, and that I knew that I made Jehovah mad. I must have looked sufficiently tortured because my mother smiled, said it was okay, but never to do it again. She said Jehovah understood the temptation and would forgive me. This is one of the few times I remember Jehovah being

9

portrayed as a God of grace and I remember the relief washing over me, as I realized my soul was not doomed to destruction at Armageddon. I went to my room to pray and tell Jehovah that I would do much better from that day forward.

For school holiday celebrations, like the Halloween parade, my Mother would pick up the five or six Jehovah's Witness kids in my school, and take us out for ice cream so that we didn't feel like we were missing out on something fun. Still, on Halloween, instead of dressing up and getting candy, we would sit inside our dark house, and pretend we weren't home. Looking back, it was pretty ironic to be the ones hiding while people knocked on OUR door. This plan to turn off the lights and hide worked out well for most years until our home Bible Study night coincided with Halloween. A group of about twenty Jehovah's Witnesses sat in my living room discussing the book of Revelation while trick or treaters loudly read the sign on our door that said "Please DO NOT Disturb! Bible study in progress." I was mortified that kids from school, who knew where I lived, would know that I was inside reading my bible while they were outside collecting candy. Nevertheless, I was also being a good little girl by not celebrating a holiday that glorified ghosts and demons, so I learned to live with the embarrassment in the name of glorifying the only true God who absolutely preferred for me to be reading my bible instead of celebrating, and eating candy with my friends.

Just like using ice cream to replace the Halloween Parade, my parents began to find other acceptable ways to substitute religious holidays. My parents' wedding anniversary was on December 31st. We began celebrating their anniversary like a family holiday, with everyone giving each other gifts. This worked out well because my parents were able to ignore the part about celebrating an unhappy marriage, and give us something to say when we returned from our school break and kids inevitably asked "what gifts did you get?" We usually spent Christmas Day skiing in Vermont and then having Chinese food for dinner. I quickly learned that many of the Jewish kids in my school had the same tradition, and that made me feel less like I was missing out, and more like I belonged, even if it was to a smaller majority of the kids at school. There was something comforting about knowing that we were not the only religion that prohibited receiving gifts on Christmas Day.

CHAPTER 3

I n Junior High I realized that Jehovah's Witnesses were also known for their racial inclusivity. I became friendly with a girl in my art class, or as friendly as you were allowed to be with a "worldly" girl. Anyone who was not a member of the true religion was considered "worldly" and therefore bad association, but somehow I must have been very comfortable with her, because I remember confiding in her that I was one of Jehovah's Witnesses. She started laughing and said "You can't be a Jehovah's Witness. They are all Black!" Apparently every Jehovah's Witness that had ever come to her door was African American. I had no idea what she was talking about, since we had people of all races and backgrounds in our congregation. I always loved the diversity of our congregation in Northern New Jersey. Even as a young child, it felt very special to me that I had a very powerful bond with people of various backgrounds. Our congregation even had an elderly interracial couple that had been married in the sixties despite great persecution. They didn't seem to like each other very much anymore, but I was always impressed that they had taken that stance against societal norms, and survived it. I felt proud to be part of an organization that called people of all races and ethnicities our brothers and sisters.

To this day, I am grateful for my parent's stance on race. Everyone was equal. This viewpoint taught me from infancy that people of all ages and races in the congregation were part of my family. I grew up without any bias against people of other cultures, races or classes. It was only other religions that had it all wrong, and would therefore be destroyed by God, but as far as Jehovah's Witnesses go, every member worldwide were all one family of true believers. It actually wasn't until much later in life that I realized that racial prejudice even existed. I know now that not being aware of racial bias was a result of my white privilege. I know how much of an issue we still have with people of other races being treated as "less than" by others, but that was not at all my experience as a child. That is one thing that Jehovah's Witnesses do right. Even if there is a natural disaster in another part of the world, the rest of the Witnesses will raise money and send in members to help them. This felt so good and right to me. I was proud to be a part of something bigger than me, a group that would take care of each other no matter what. That ability to belong to a tight knit group of people is such a gift, but it's also a curse because the Witnesses will use it to keep you from leaving. The risk of being shunned from this group that is considered a family is so great that they can use it as a bribe to make you stay a part of the organization, even if you question aspects of the religion.

In order to be approved to go to other countries after natural disasters and help rebuild homes, and our buildings of worship, you had to be a part of the Regional Building Committee. I was thrilled to be accepted as a part of this committee when I was fourteen. The Regional Building Committee was a group of Witnesses whose main purpose was to build Kingdom Halls, which were our places of worship. My uncle was an elder and one of the heads of the RBC. I was so excited to be approved to go on my first project. My uncle was going to pick me up, drive me to the building site, and help me get set up with a crew that would teach me a building skill. The morning of my first build, I woke up with a fever of 104. I had chills, nausea, and my body ached. I also had tiny circular rashes all over my body. There was no way I could go to the build. My mother took me to the Doctor and I was diagnosed with Lyme Disease. I was given a round of antibiotics, and within a few weeks, I was back to my old self, but I was devastated to have missed my first opportunity to work on a build. It would be months before I would be approved to go on another project, and for a fourteen year old girl who wanted nothing more than to be able to help my brothers and sisters internationally after any kind of natural disaster, the wait felt like forever.

Eventually, I was allowed to attend a local project where they were building a new Kingdom Hall. After very minimal training, I joined the HVAC crew. I received informal, on the job training, and learned quickly how to install ductwork in the ceilings. I loved swinging myself up into the rafters and showing the "brothers" that I could do whatever they could do. As a woman in the organization, we are taught to be submissive, and to listen to the guidance and direction of the men in the organization. This ability to do manual labor, and keep up with the "brothers" fueled my feminist fire. It was the one place in the organization where a woman was praised for being independent, educated, and even a touch masculine. That little taste of equality, even if it was only alive in the rafters of our unfinished houses of worship, was so inspiring to me.

CHAPTER 4

Growing up in the organization, women are not allowed to give sermons from the platform. My father, however, was a man with a prominent position in the congregation. As such, he was asked to travel to different local congregations to be a guest speaker at the Sunday morning sermon. Each Elder and Ministerial Servant (like a Junior Elder or Elder light), was assigned different outlines of sermons to give. They were called "talks" like they would be given in a conversational manner, but really they are just "talking" to the audience from a podium on stage. My father drew the short straw, and was assigned to travel to different Kingdom Halls on Sundays and give the sermon about what fornication entailed, and how it ultimately led to destruction by God at Armageddon. For a God of Love, the Witnesses focus an awful lot on his ability to destroy people. My father would give this sermon several times a year, and our family would sit in the audience, with this message being indoctrinated over and over again. In the eyes of the cult, any touching of the genitals by any body part (yours or other people's) was considered fornication. As a child, hearing this message over and over again, I got the firm and concrete message that genital touching was a sin that would lead to death at the hands of our very prude Heavenly Father.

This message would have been harmful enough for a healthy child to hear over and over again, but it was extremely detrimental, and life shattering to me, as a four year old child with an unexplained kidney disorder. For three years, I had recurring bladder and kidney infections with unexplained origin. About halfway through this period of illnesses, I remember my Pediatrician asking my Mother to talk privately without me in the room. My mother stormed out of the Doctor's office after their meeting and told me that the Doctor believed I was attention seeking, and causing my own illness by holding my urine. The Doctor told her to scare me by telling me I would need to go to the hospital every time I got sick, so they could discern whether or not this was a real or made up illness. In the end, being sick was something I could not control, no matter how much they tried to scare me straight. I was hospitalized several times with fevers that raged into the night, and kidney infections that wouldn't subside. As part of the journey to figure out the problem I was having, the Doctor ordered a test called a VCUG. I believe I was about six at the time. For this test, I would have to drink a large amount of fluid, lay on an x-ray table, and the technician would take pictures of my bladder, as I peed on the table. Despite my mother's pleas, and the frustration of the technologist trying to perform the scan, I could not soil myself on the table. The idea of being dirty in public went against my core belief system that I had to be clean and good for God to love me. To do what they were asking felt unsurvivable. So, I didn't.

In addition to the failed VCUG, I had several catheters, and ultrasounds, of my bladder and pelvis. For each of these tests, I remembered my father's words. I wholeheartedly believed that if I let the Doctor or technician see, or touch my private parts, God would destroy me. So I would fight. I would refuse the test, or struggle to get free. This would mean that my Mother had to hold me down so that the test could be performed. As a child, this confused me, because my Mother knew what fornication was, and yet she was holding me down so that these men could touch my genitals. In my little girl brain, I assumed this meant that my Mother wanted me to be destroyed by God. If my Mother wanted me to be destroyed, I must be worthless and unlovable. This belief system took deep root over those years of illness. My self worth deteriorated, and my self loathing expanded into every cell of my body.

Eventually, we found a surgeon who determined that the tube that connected my bladder to my kidney was too narrow, causing urine to back up and get trapped in the kidney. This was the cause of my recurring infections, and it needed to be corrected surgically. This surgery was done by making a large scar from hip to hip across my seven year old abdomen. After surgery, I was afraid the doctor would want to examine the catheter coming out of my private parts, again a sin against God, so alone in the hospital room, I pulled the catheter out myself, with the balloon still fully inflated, causing permanent damage to my urethra. To this day, I am jealous of my best friend for having a urine stream accurate enough to write her name in the snow as she pees. This is the power of religious trauma. This is how religious trauma and cult belief systems begin to cause complete emotional and physical damage. I, as an innocent child, would rather pull a large balloon through a small whole in my urethra, hours after bladder surgery, than disrespect Jehovah God by letting a doctor remove the catheter in a safe and sterile way.

As I began to heal from surgery, my Mother turned her attention to my complete gut destruction resulting from three years of constant antibiotics. She put me on a "candida cleanse" which consisted of no refined sugar, gluten, vinegar, fruit, or dairy. So now I was not only the kid in the cult, but the kid in the cult with the weird food at lunch time. I remember a kid picking up a pine cone from the playground at recess and saying "This is what Megan eats!". Trauma like this happens to every kid. We blow it off by saying "kids will be kids". But where does that hurt go? My body was still healing from the infections, surgeries and antibiotics, so again these feelings of isolation and worthlessness got shoved deep down into my scars as it healed. It would be almost fifteen years before I began to understand how this trauma, and my emotions, affected my physical body, but we will get to that later.

CHAPTER 5

As I continued to grow up and enter my tween years, I made a promise to God that I would make up for all of the "fornication" I had allowed to happen to my body as a child. I would be perfect. I would be an example. I would praise him and be good. For this reason, I was the first of all of my friends to get baptized as a Jehovah's Witness, at the age of ten. I was not aware of what this "spiritual contract" would mean. I did not know that this decision to get baptized as one of Jehovah's Witnesses, a decision I made as a ten year old child, would mean that I would lose my entire family, and everyone I knew, when I left the organization.

Even after baptism, I did not feel worthy. I remembered the feeling of control I had when I lost weight on the "candida cleanse" after my surgery. That feeling, along with watching my mother (and let's be real... most women in America) strive to stay thin, created the belief system that part of being good and perfect was to be as small as possible. We were taught that women are to be submissive to men. That we were not allowed to have a voice within the congregation. If we dared to have an "original thought" in the presence of a man, we were not allowed to share that thought without wearing a head covering. Women were not allowed to hold any position of authority in the congregation. They were not allowed to give sermons, or be a part of "shepherding" the congregation. With all of these constant admonitions to be small, or invisible, I began to fear the fact that I was a very tall girl. Frantic to follow the rules, and shrink to be obedient, I started my first diet at the age of eleven. I had gained a significant amount of weight once my Mother took me off of the restrictive diet to heal my gut, and I felt burdened. I felt shameful. So I began restricting what I ate until the pounds came off again. This was the beginning of several decades of disordered eating.

By the time I turned thirteen, I was five foot, ten inches tall, and one hundred and forty five pounds. I read that this was the exact height and weight of Cindy Crawford at the peak of her modeling career, so I decided that these dimensions were acceptable for a submissive female servant of God. The organization was big on the belief that women were beautiful vessels to be cherished and taken care of, but also that those vessels couldn't do much more than be beautiful and take care of a household. This idea of a fragile but beautiful female image was repeatedly emphasized in our religious literature and in sermons from the platform. Submissiveness, being humble, and teachable, and not too flashy, were the required traits for a "sister" in the congregation. However, she was also expected to maintain her appearance, while also demonstrating humility, so that she could be valued as a treasure.

My mother allowed me to begin wearing makeup, and trade my glasses for contact lenses when I turned thirteen. I felt so proud to be maturing, and I was learning that changing my appearance was one way to get external validation and attention. The down side of this was that I started getting attention from "brothers" who were much older than me. That year, one "brother" in his twenties told me that he had been watching me grow up since I was a child, and he would be interested in courting me when I was old enough. Another Elder, who was my father's age, pulled me aside. He asked me to sit with him, alone, in a quiet area of the Kingdom Hall. He looked deeply into my eyes and told me that he saw me growing from a child into a woman, and he wanted me to know that he noticed it happening. It felt grimy, and dirty, and my intuition screamed that something about this conversation wasn't right, but he was a respected Elder, and my parent's favorite person, so I told no one.

Later that year, we had been chosen as a model family to be part of the program and take the stage at a convention of Jehovah's Witnesses. During these twice annual conventions, thousands of Jehovah's Witnesses would flock to a large convention center and spend three to four days, eight hours a day, sitting and listening to sermon after sermon. It was a huge honor to be selected to be a part of the program. As one of the head Elders, my father was often chosen to present at these conventions, but it was rare that our whole family would be involved. As part of this commitment to be a part of the program, we would speak in front of more than three thousand people at Nassau Coliseum. Despite my ever present self loathing, I felt a glimmer of hope that if we were chosen to perform as an example, I must not be the complete shit storm of a human I had convinced myself I was. Most importantly, I was confident in my choice of attire. It had to be approved by the elders, and considered modest. My dress was long, almost down to my ankles, but tied around the waist showing off my recently blossomed figure.

This was my debut. We were going on stage as a family, and were supposed to be giving these three thousand Jehovah's Witnesses a glimpse into our perfect family routine of morning Bible discussion. We were called upon to paint a perfect picture of a Christian family. We were chosen because my father was the Presiding Overseer, or head honcho, of the congregation. My mother was balancing her duties as a Christian wife and mother with a commitment to volunteer sixty hours per month finding "right hearted ones" and teaching them about the Bible, God's requirements, and why our religion was the only one that counts. She would drive us to school, clean the house, have dinner on the table, and save the souls of many. My older sister was sixteen. She was painfully shy, and extraordinarily brilliant. I didn't ask her at the time, but I'm sure that speaking in front of all of those people was sheer torture for her. But for the sake of our sacred duty, she complied. The speaker gave his cue, we walked up on stage, making sure we didn't trip, our posture was perfect, and God forbid, we didn't flash too much leg as we sat down on the chairs provided. It was meticulously rehearsed. We shared a scripture, discussed its modern day applications, showed how my sister Gabriella and I were instantly better children as a result of this guidance and direction, how my mother was being used by God to rear us in his wisdom, and my father was the ideal family head, providing for us physically and spiritually. We nailed it. Five minutes later, we were spiritual rock stars. We were the family everyone should strive to be. In case of an emergency, God would probably save us first.

I was struggling hard to be a perfect child, both in front of the witnesses, and also at school so that I could be an example of what a "good Christian" looks like. So with my head and heart in the right place, I started my seventh grade year by walking into my Spanish level one class, and sat down next to a kid named Jacob. Jacob was everything I was not. He was a boy with long, dark hair. He wore his pants so baggy that they were falling half way down his butt, and oversized sweatshirts that seemed to swallow up this already skinny teenage boy. Jacob gave zero fucks. I don't know how else to describe him. He didn't care about rules, or propriety. He did what he wanted, when he wanted, and somehow teachers and students still liked him. He carried a pillow around with him from class to class. When kids would ask him why he had a pillow he would say "oh, it's for nunya." Inevitably, they would reply "Nunya?" He would smirk and say "yeah, NUNYA business." In a tone that made it clear he wasn't going to be answering any more questions.

One day Jacob borrowed a pen from the Spanish teacher. She handed it over hesitantly saying "You can borrow this, but you HAVE to give it back, because it's my very favorite pen." A few minutes later she excitedly asked Jacob "Don't you just love that pen?" And he replied "Yes! It's orgasmic!". The teacher's face got very red and she started to giggle. I sat there in literal awe of this boy. He didn't follow any of the "rules" I had for how to get people to approve of you, and therefore like you. He said whatever came to his mind, and this authority figure thought he was hilarious! We also had two kids named Neil and Bob in our class who sat next to each other. Every time the teacher paired kids up to work together, Neil and Bob would be assigned to work together and Jacob would yell out "KNEEL and BOB". All of the kids knew he was referring to oral sex, but it went right over the teacher's head until one day, he shouted "KNEEL and BOB", she turned bright red and started laughing, covering her face with her shirt so that we couldn't see her reaction.

Jacob could do that. He could be entirely inappropriate, even with people in positions of authority, and he could get away with it. I remember wanting to be around Jacob as much as I could. I envied him. I felt like here I was, wasting so much time and energy trying to please everyone, especially authority figures, and here was this kid who would never even think to try to please people. He was just one hundred percent authentic. I longed to live in a world where I could be like him. But since I was not allowed to associate with any of the "worldly" kids outside of school, this was as much as I would get to know about Jacob in those early years. Still, it was a feeling I would never forget, a crush based entirely on admiring the hell out of someone being so true to who they were, despite any social norms. In truth, I admired Jacob more than I had ever admired anyone before.

Around this same time, my parents began allowing us to travel around to meet other Jehovah's Witness kids from neighboring congregations. My sister usually chose to stay home, but, being an extrovert, I loved meeting other kids that were considered "good association" and often drove several hours to go to witness approved parties or events. The first time I met Justin, he was sitting on a blanket under a tree, with a group of boys that belonged to a congregation in New York. We were at a small town festival called the Montgomery Day Parade. He was wearing a choker type necklace, and his hair was longer on one side than the other so that when he looked up at me, and gave me his signature smirk, he was peeking out from under that mop of hair. I was still thirteen years old. I knew two things right away, that he was way cooler than I was, and that he was magnetic. It was similar to that feeling I had had around Jacob, except that I also felt this immediate connection to him. I felt, instantaneously, like he was mine, like I had known him my whole life, and that he was trouble. Everything else about that day is a blur except for that moment, the first time he looked at me. For the next year or so, we had a relationship full of a constant push and pull. The force of the universe pulling us together, and the straight jacket of the cult we both belonged to pulling us apart. It was the stuff young adult novels are made of, teenage hormones, forbidden love, and undeniable soulmates.

I honestly am not sure that all humans get to experience that feeling. It's hard to describe what I felt the moment I saw him, that feeling of being pleasantly on fire. The moment I recognized a piece of my soul in another human. The moment that felt so right, so alive, and so forbidden. Some part of me knew, even then, that the purpose of life is to follow that aliveness, and realize that any rules against it are where the lessons for this lifetime lie.

After a few months of talking online, and hanging out sporadically, which was as much as two kids too young to drive could see each other, Justin broke up with me. It was my first taste of heartbreak. We were messaging each other through AOL instant messenger. I read those words on the screen over and over again. He said that he wanted to wait to have a relationship with me until we were both old enough to grow a relationship that could last long term. I believed his whole spiel until, as any fourteen year old boy would do, he began dating a girl we both knew, with much bigger boobs, a few weeks later. For many years, Justin would be the only guy to have ever broken my heart. Some part of me resolved to never let that happen again. I was proud of my almost decade long track record, that the only boy who had ever broken my heart was when I was fourteen, but really, this truth just highlights the fact that after he broke my heart, any time I would get any kind of inkling that someone was going to leave me, I would leave them first. Over the years, this dysfunctional pattern caused myself, and many men in my life, a great deal of pain.

Justin and I ended our "relationship" during the summer after my eighth grade year. That fall, I started my freshman year of high school. I was still playing the part of the chaste and true minister's daughter, saving the world from hedonism, and providing a shining example to others. The only problem was that now I had not only captured the attention of "true Christians", I was also fresh meat to the "worldly" high school boys. As very pure and wholesome Christians, I had never had the talk about "the birds and the bees" with my parents. In fact, we rarely spoke about anything of substance at all. We were German, and conservative, and probably would have been Republican if we were allowed to show our allegiance to anything other than God's Kingdom. Ours was a family where there was a surplus of religion, and our needs were always attended to, but it was also devoid of emotion. The Bible says "the heart is treacherous" and the Germans say "if it's uncomfortable, sweep it under the rug". So we played our roles, and lived life with as little emotional connection as possible.

All of this was well and good until I met Steven Murphy. Steven was a senior, and a member of the football team. He was big and strong, outgoing, and most importantly, he looked out for my sister. Around this time, my sister was diagnosed with Social Phobia Disorder and there were very few people that she considered a friend. As Jehovah's Witnesses, we were not allowed to socialize outside of school hours with anyone who wasn't also a Jehovah's Witness, because "bad association spoils useful habits" and if you are not a member of the cult, you are not "good association". I later learned that this is how cults work. They isolate you from the outside world, in order to maintain their brainwashing. Anyone who thinks differently than the cult poses a threat to your continued loyalty to the group. So although we couldn't have non-witness or "worldly" friends outside of school hours, we used the time at school to develop friendships as best we could with our fellow classmates. Then we went home, and hung out with our "real friends", also known as our "brothers and sisters" in the organization. Gabriella was two and a half years older than me, but her Social Phobia, in combination with my blatant gregariousness, made me her protector. I was her spokeswoman, her social director, and I was always on the lookout for ways to diffuse any situation that could become uncomfortable for her. When I saw Steven befriending my sister, and looking out for her, I was immediately drawn to him as a person. He was tall, handsome, popular, and my co-pilot in the mission to save my sister.

Of course, since you can't even be friends with a "non-witness", you can imagine their stance on dating outside of our religion. The congregation held firm to the tenant that "you may not become unevenly yoked with an unbeliever". You also may not have sex before marriage, and so, to hedge our bets, you may not date until you are past the "bloom of youth". This means you are not supposed to date until you are capable of choosing a marriage mate without basing that decision solely on the immediate need to have sex. Breaking these rules could lead to immediate, and complete shunning from the congregation. So, Steven was a conundrum. I couldn't date him, I couldn't develop feelings for him, and I certainly couldn't flirt with him. But there was something about the attention he gave me that felt like a drug. It was a mix of affection and compassion. It felt like I was being seen for the first time. In those moments, where he paid me attention, I felt like maybe I wasn't totally worthless. I was a freshman, and this popular senior boy got a sparkle in his eye when he came near me. I must have some kind of redeeming quality for him to give me the time of day. Steven gave me the attention that I had never received at home, and how could he be a "bad association" when he looked after my sister and protected her? How could he be bad, when he looked at me like I was the game winning touchdown? And how could he be bad when the way he touched my waist as I walked by him in the hallway made me feel like I needed to go home and say a prayer. Steven Murphy was either the work of the Devil, or the best thing that had ever happened to me. I knew, despite my perfect reputation, and my title of Princess Goody Two Shoes, I would do whatever I needed to do to spend time with him.

Over the course of that year, Steven got the message that I was his number one fan. Perhaps it was the way I blushed when he said hello, or the fact that I told everyone who would listen how amazing I thought he was. Maybe it was the fact that I giggled at every word he said. You see, as a Jehovah's Witness, who is not allowed to date except for the purpose of finding a suitable marriage mate, neither my parents, nor my social phobic older sister had taught me how to have any game at all. So, I blatantly and shamefully adored him. I needed him to notice me, so I did what any fourteen year old minister's daughter would do... I hid mini skirts in my backpack, and changed in the bathroom once I got to school. I started to walk with a little more swagger, and I enjoyed the attention I was getting, not just from Steven, but from the opposite sex in general. My spiritual light was growing dimmer and my freak flag was starting to fly. Then one day it happened. I got the news that someone said Steven told them that he had to "be careful" around me, because I was young and attractive, and could get him in trouble. Having no concept of what kind of "trouble" an eighteen year old boy could be worried about with a fourteen year old girl, I filtered this comment down to "man, I think he likes me!" At that moment I was sure that we would fall in love, he would convert to the only true religion, we would get married, and live happily ever after. After all, that's what people who like each other do, right? Hold hands, get married, and preach the Word of God. All I had to do was let him know the attraction was mutual, and the rest would fall right into place. How could what I was doing be wrong when, in the end, I would probably recruit him into the ranks of the true religion, and save his soul? So I squelched my ever present guilt, and concocted a plan.

I figured the most important part of falling in love was having time alone together, but this was absolutely against the rules. Even if two members of the congregation are old enough to marry, they can only date with a chaperone. My being fourteen, and wanting to be alone with a "worldly" eighteen year old, was a definite no no. I decided that in order to get around this, I would invite Steven over to the house where I was babysitting, after the little girl had gone to bed. I knew that it was wrong, but I was running out of time before he left for college, and his attention was like a drug I was not willing to give up. He was the only thing that made me feel like I had any value. When I offered this invitation, I had no idea that a typical eighteen year old boy would construe an invitation to a house without parents as a sexual invitation. I had worn a casual knee length dress to go babysit. It was cute enough by worldly standards, appropriate for a girl my age, but also cult approved because it was knee length, and therefore, modest.

Steven came to the house, and as he was walking in the door, he gave me his signature smirk that made my stomach flutter. We sat down on the couch and talked for a few minutes, and then he leaned in to kiss me. This was everything I had ever wanted. He must love me. He must want to be with me forever. But my joy was very short-lived, because after just a few seconds, I felt Steven's hand on my knee begin to move up my thigh. I started to panic. This was not at all what I expected to happen, and I didn't know what to do. I froze. At that moment, my senses became extremely acute. I was extremely aware that he was much taller and stronger than I was, that there was a little girl sleeping upstairs that I could not wake, and that I did not know how to stop what was happening. But if I didn't stop him, I would be shunned from the congregation, and destroyed by God. Steven removed my underwear, and roughly moved his fingers inside me. Still, I stayed silent. Frozen. I was not giving any signals that I was okay with what was happening, but I also never said no. I had no voice at all. Eventually he stopped what he was doing, and I reached down to pull my underwear back up and got up off of the couch. He asked me to give him a tour of the house, and I was so relieved that he had stopped touching me, that I moved numbly from the living room into the kitchen. Steven pointed to a door on the side of the kitchen and said "what's down there?" I said "I don't know. The basement?" He took my hand and walked me downstairs.

At this point, I felt simultaneously relieved to be farther away from the little girl sleeping upstairs, and terrified to be entering a dark basement with this guy who had gone from my hero to a potential predator in the matter of a few minutes. Steven lifted me up onto a workbench and began touching me again. Again I stayed silent. At some point, he had undone his pants because they were now around his ankles. He reached out, grabbed my hand and put it on his penis. I pulled it away. As he put the tip of his penis on my vagina he whispered "I want to fuck you" and my paralysis vanished. My mind went from blank and numb to terrified. I switched into fight or flight. If he was going to do this to me, I was going to go down fighting. Making Steven happy was no longer at the top of my list of most important things. I jumped off of the table, and walked to the stairs. I was acutely aware that I didn't know where my underwear was, and now my "modest" t-shirt dress felt much too revealing. I told him he had to go. He pulled up his pants and left.

Once I saw his car driving safely out of the driveway, I went upstairs to check on the little girl I was babysitting. Thankfully, she was still sound asleep. I went back downstairs and cried. I called my friend, another "worldly" girl from school, and told her what had happened. She taught me how to clean myself up to avoid a bladder infection. She also told me that I needed to be more direct next time. I was shocked by her belief that saying "no" and telling someone something they didn't want to hear was always an option. That concept felt very foreign to me, but also filled me with guilt that maybe I should have spoken up after all, and this really was all my fault.

When the parents returned home from their date night, the father drove me home. I was mortified to be wearing a dress, and to be sitting in his car without any underwear on. I never found them. Later, I learned that Steven left the house, took my underwear, and went right to a party where he showed all of the boys in the Senior class, and told them that I was a tease. Me. The minister's daughter. The girl who had always done everything right. In one night, without even having sex, I had gone from complete prude to a slut. I felt shame in every cell of my body. I knew, right away, that I had to confess. I knew I would have to report my sins to the elders, and that this one decision to trust Steven, could change my life forever.

The next morning, I called my father's best friend, another Elder in our congregation. We will call him Paul. I told Paul that I needed to talk. We had church services three times a week, and one of them was that night, so he said we could chat after the meeting. Paul then called my parents to inform them of the meeting. My parents both walked into my room and asked me what happened. I remember laughing nervously. I couldn't stop smiling. I was so anxious, and so embarrassed, and my face was not conveying the amount of remorse I felt. It was as if my soul had left my body, and any semblance of a normal reaction had left with it. I told my parents that I got myself into trouble with a boy while I was babysitting. My mother's first reaction was to yell at me saying that I may have ruined our chance at going to

Germany. Our family had been picked to be representatives of the United States at an International Convention of Jehovah's Witnesses. Only exceptional families could attend these conventions, and if I was deemed a sinner, our family would not meet the standards required to attend. So with the fear of everyone I knew having to shun me, the fear of losing this privilege for my parents, and the fear of God destroying me for what I had done, I went into the back room with Elder Paul to confess my sins. For the record, this was the same elder who had pulled me aside shortly after I turned thirteen to tell me that he noticed the change of a girl becoming a woman, happening to me. Now I was alone in a room with this man, confessing what had happened with Steven. He seemed taken back and said "This was not at all what I expected you to say. I thought you were going to say that you wanted to go on a missionary trip, and your parents thought you were too young. I did not expect that you would need a judicial committee." I sat there embarrassed, with shame seeping out of every pore.

A few days later, I was pulled into an official judicial committee. This is a group of three elders who will hear you confess your sins, and determine if you will be shunned or allowed to remain a part of the congregation. I had already lived through the hell of that night when it first happened, and then lived through it again when I told Paul what had happened. Now, I had to relive it another time as I explained, in detail, what had happened to three of my father's closest friends. These were men who regularly spent time at our home, who I saw several times a week, and I was sitting across from them alone, without my parents. I was a child who had just been traumatized and they were asking me questions like "who took off your underwear, him or you?" "How many fingers did he use when he was penetrating you?" I answered their questions over and over again and finally I was allowed to go home and await my sentencing. The next day Paul called again and asked me the same questions, making me relive every detail of that night for the fourth time. He said "I think we get the picture".

Even now, decades later, thinking about the events of that night and all of the times I had to recount the event to be sentenced by the religion, gives me a panic attack. My hands start to shake and sweat, my chest gets tight, and I can't breathe. I learned later that the events of that night triggered PTSD, and the fact that these men made me keep reliving these events over and over made my brain handle it like C-PTSD, or complex PTSD, where a traumatic event happens over and over again. PTSD is very hard to treat, and C-PTSD is almost impossible to recover from completely. That progression of damage happened because of the Jehovah's Witnesses and how they handle reports of sexual assault, especially in children. Unfortunately, I am not the only one this happened to. The witnesses take Matthew 18:16 very literally when it says that "every matter may be established by the testimony of two or three witnesses." So if there wasn't another witness besides the victim, then in their eyes, sexual assault didn't happen. Worldwide, within the Jehovah's Witness organization, thousands of children have come forward to the elders, as we are instructed to do, and confided in them that they have been sexually assaulted. Many of these victims, including myself, were told that they were not allowed to speak about the incident with anyone outside of the judicial committee to avoid embarrassment by the victim, and the organization they are a part of. We were also told that if the events did become "public" among the congregation, then our punishment could be increased from a private matter to a public one, where our sins and resulting punishment would be shared with the congregation from the platform during one of our meetings. We were traumatized, then re-traumatized in the judicial committees, then invalidated, and finally silenced.

As all of these events were happening, some part of myself, deep in my stomach, was saying "This is not the true religion. This is not how God would want this to be handled. Something about this is very wrong." A few days later, Paul came over and sat down at the kitchen table with my mother and me. He said "We have decided that Megan is not at fault, and there will be no punishment for this offense." My mother was relieved because we would be able to go to Germany. At some point Paul must have told my mother that what happened was sexual assault because she came into my room, sat down next to me on my bed with a stiff arm around my shoulders and said "that must have been awful to go through alone." I said it was, and that was it. That was the end of the conversation. My mother got up and left the room, and we never spoke of the incident again. Although I still had this gnawing feeling that this was not the true religion, I was a child, living in my parents' household and had no choice but to continue on as a Jehovah's Witness. Some part of me also thought that Jehovah had shown the Elders the truth, and the fact that I was not punished, showed that God was present in the proceedings. So I decided that I would continue on as a Jehovah's Witness, and be the very best Christian I could be, so that I would never have to experience a judicial committee again in my life. However, as I tried to be "good enough" and rebuild my relationship with God, I also felt the loneliest I had ever been in my life and I felt a deep self hatred that began to envelop me even further.

After my judicial committee with the elders, and my family's trip to the International Convention of Jehovah's Witnesses in Germany, I hit a new emotional low. Without Steven's attention, I began to feel invisible and worthless again. I would hide these feelings by being very social. I would organize groups of Witness kids to get together and hang out so that I wouldn't be alone. Being busy and having something to do allowed me to drown out the negative feelings that I was unlovable.

CHAPTER 6

S omewhere in these years, my Mother sought out
therapy for my sister to try to combat her ever
increasing social phobia. As part of her therapy, they
began trying different drugs to help her fight her anxiety.
Some of these drugs caused my sister to gain weight, and
some would make her stay in bed for days at a time. One day
I walked into the kitchen and saw my mom standing at the
kitchen sink filling the dishwasher. Her hands were shaking.
Being the mediator of the family, I asked her what was wrong.
She said that she was concerned that Gabriella's anxiety was
becoming unbearable for her but she also thought Gabriella's
depression on the medications was getting worse. Jehovah's
Witnesses believe that if you die, after Armageddon, you will
be resurrected to everlasting life on a paradise earth. That day
my mother told me that the Bible says if you commit suicide,
you will not be resurrected. As Gabriella's depression got
worse, my mother was facing every parent's worst nightmare
that Gabriella would take her life, and none of us would ever
see her again. This conversation was the second time in my
life that I had a full body "knowing" that the beliefs of
Jehovah's Witnesses were not the "true religion" and that
these beliefs were so far removed from the "God of love" that
we were meant to be worshiping. I began to resent this God

that would make me feel so worthless as a young child, and now would punish someone for actions they may take as a result of a chemical imbalance in the brain. What God would want a mother shaking at the kitchen sink, simultaneously worried about her daughter's mental health, and also her eternal future? The pit in my stomach grew larger that day as I knew, once again, on a cellular level, that this religion I was being raised in was a lie.

With this growing resentment towards God, and my need to find love and attention wherever I could, I turned again to getting attention from guys, since that came naturally for me. I had just turned fifteen, and I looked much older than I was. Some of my friends in the congregation were a little older, and had started getting their driver's licenses, so our group of approved associations (other Witnesses) got bigger than just the kids in our local town. We started hanging out with other witnesses from different congregations. That was how I met a twenty one year old guy named Brad. Brad came on very strong. I don't even remember how we started dating, or the beginning stages of our relationship. I just remember older girls in the congregation pulling me aside and saying that Brad was a catch, and asking how I was able to get him to notice me when I was only fifteen. This attention gave me some validation and made me feel like maybe there was something of value about me. So I threw myself wholeheartedly into the relationship.

In the next few months Brad began planting little seeds of insecurity into my head. He would say things like "you are very pretty, but if you could lose ten pounds in your butt you would be a knockout". He would give me backwards compliments that would undermine my self esteem and make me question even more if I was really good enough. I confided in him about what had happened with Stephen and he said that proved that I needed him to tell me what to do, because the decisions I made on my own were immoral and would get me destroyed at Armageddon. Since there is no sex before marriage among Jehovah's Witnesses, and Brad was twenty one, he began insisting that we would get married once I turned sixteen. When I told him I didn't want to get married that young, and that I assumed we would date until I was at least eighteen, he said that I couldn't expect him to wait that long to have sex. He insisted that because of what happened with Stephen, I was damaged goods, and no other man in the congregation would want me.

As we got closer to my sixteenth birthday, I began to dread what would happen if I didn't marry Brad, and I figured my best bet was to tell my parents what was going on so that they would put an end to the relationship for me. That was exactly what happened. My mother was appalled that a man so much older than me would have taken advantage of me, but other than forbidding me to see Brad again, we never spoke of the relationship after that.

The events of those two years changed me to my core. The belief system that I was unlovable, dirty, used, and useless began to dig down and grow roots. I was tall and young, and people would often tell me that I was beautiful, but I would look into the mirror and cry because I was sure that I was too ugly to leave the house. I allowed myself to fall apart in the quiet and privacy of my own room, but in public, I maintained my identity as the minister's daughter, sister's helper, and comedian charged with breaking the ever present family tension. This dichotomy became very natural. I could easily split myself open and put on the appearance of whomever the people around me needed me to be. I figured that if no one knew the real me, then when they decided I was unlovable, I could tell myself that it was because they didn't really know me. This was my first suit of armor in protecting myself from judgment. They couldn't reject me if they didn't know who I really was.

Fortunately, over the next several years I would grow friendships within the congregation that were very beneficial. I had a loving and caring boyfriend named Casey, who taught me that I was good, and kind, and worthy of love. He treated me like gold, and loved spending time with me. Just being around Casey improved my self esteem, and made me feel like someone cared about me. We dated for nearly two years, and he was my very favorite person. Unfortunately, the first time Casey told me he loved me, I completely shut down. Having never heard those words before, from my parents or grandparents or anyone related to me, I felt extremely uncomfortable with them. I mistook my severe discomfort with the words "I love you" to mean that I didn't love Casey back, but that wasn't the truth. He was a wonderful man, who I deeply cared about, but I did not know how to show him love in return. I ended my relationship with Casey, even though I loved him, because I didn't know how to be with someone who loved me. The thought of trying to express love was too scary. So I let him go.

After my break up with Casey, I realized that something was really wrong with me. I figured the only people who could explain why I was uncomfortable with emotion were the people who raised me to be that way. As someone who will do almost anything to avoid conflict, I was not excited about broaching this topic with my parents, but I knew that if I ever wanted to be in a healthy relationship, I needed two get to the bottom of why the word love made me so uncomfortable.

I approached my mother, and asked her why she and Dad never told my sister and I that they loved us. If my mother was a bottle of kerosine, that question was the match that lit the kerosine on fire. She got red in the face and that vein in her neck that meant I had really messed up started throbbing more than I had ever seen it bulge before. She got extremely angry and began to yell saying "Do you think anyone has ever said that to me?!"

My mother was raised by wonderful parents, but they were conservative, German, and didn't share emotion well. She grew up without an example of how to be outwardly affectionate with her children. Her needs were always met, and she was loved, but she was never given the words of affirmation to help her internalize that love. Around this time my father confided in me that he had left home at the age of sixteen. I asked him what his mother, my Grandmother, had to say about that. He answered, "I don't think she noticed." So neither of my parents had warm and fuzzy childhoods. I realize now, as a mother myself, that my parents did the very best they could. It wasn't enough to prevent me from deep wounds that would haunt me for the rest of my life, but it was the very best they could do. I think about this often in my own parenting journey. Our natural instinct is to parent our children the way we were parented. It is our choice if we want to pass on that parenting style to our children or if we want to change it, but to change it takes considerable work and healing on the part of the parent. To this day, I strive to heal myself enough that I can prevent my girls from having any of these wounds themselves, although even as I write that, I know that no parent is perfect, and to try to raise our children without inflicting any emotional wounds is an impossible task. Still, I think the most important part of parenting is to let our children know that no matter what they do, and no matter how we respond to what they do, they are loved unconditionally. I tell my children every day that they are loved the maximum amount, just for being my children, and that nothing they can do or say will ever decrease the amount that I love them. I hope that constant reminder is enough to make up for all of the mistakes I make parenting them along the way.

CHAPTER 7

At age sixteen, I was able to graduate from high school early, and started to think about college. Of all of the adults in my life that I really loved and respected, I held my Aunt Karen at the top of that list. She was a nurse who always made me feel loved, special and important. She was always happy and laughing, and she took an interest in me. She would ask me questions about my life and school, and she made me feel like I might indeed have a little bit of value. I wanted to make other people feel the way my Aunt Karen made me feel, so I told my mother that I wanted to be a nurse.

As a Jehovah's Witness in the late nineties, college was looked down upon. The theory was that Armageddon was going to come any day, so why would you waste your money on higher education that might lead you away from the true religion, when what you SHOULD be doing is preaching to others. The witnesses believe that Armageddon will come once every person on earth has had the chance to hear "the truth" and accept or deny it. We were told that the faster we preached, and the more people we converted, the sooner God would step in, destroy evil, and return the planet to a paradise earth under the rule of Jesus Christ and the 144,000 anointed ones who would be co-rulers with him in heaven.

It would also be unacceptable for a Jehovah's Witness to live on campus at a University because then you would be surrounded by "bad association" that would increase the chance that you would be swayed by their beliefs and leave "the truth". So, if I was going to be allowed to attend college at all, I would most definitely have to live at home with my parents while I went. That being said, college options were limited, but I was just grateful that I was allowed to attend college at all. Fortunately, my parents did believe that it was important for me to be able to support myself as a single person if I decided not to get married and so they were supportive of my pursuing some kind of career in the medical field.

I got a full scholarship to Fairleigh Dickinson University for their Physical Therapy program. Although it wasn't the nursing career that I wanted, it was free, and close enough to home that I could commute, and therefore, it was good enough. This program only had thirty spots available, but I was accepted and so excited to begin. Out of all thirty of us who started the program, only four of us graduated. The rest of the people failed out, or decided they couldn't maintain the amount of course work and studying required, and switched to easier majors. The amount of pressure in this program was extremely intense and I began suffering from stomach ulcers. I didn't know what was causing the stomach pain, and I certainly didn't have time to take care of it, so I coped by limiting what I ate. I figured that if I cut out enough kinds of food, I would eventually eliminate whatever was causing the problem.

As an unintentional consequence, I began to see that limiting calories and losing weight made me feel powerful. It was something that I could control in a time when everything seemed so out of control. I stopped eating all sugar and gluten and basically anything at all that might make me gain weight. I began to live off of coffee, which in hindsight, was the worst thing I could do for my ulcers. Even in college, my ADD had not been diagnosed, and so I medicated myself with caffeine. I found that when I drank coffee, I wasn't hungry anymore, and I could focus on memorizing all of the bones and muscles and exercises that I needed to memorize. I graduated from this program in 2001 with a 3.95 GPA. One of my professors sat me down and said "You are the valedictorian of this program. You would be doing yourself a huge disservice if you do not go on to get your Doctorate in Physical Therapy." These Doctorate programs were just starting to come onto the scene, and I wanted, more than anything, to continue my studies.

I sat down with my parents and told them that even though my program was coming to an end, I wasn't ready to be done with college. I told them that I wanted to continue, and that I still had scholarship money I could use to keep studying. My father said he understood where I was coming from, and that he thought it was a good idea. My mother broke down crying. At this point she was a Pioneer which is what we call full time volunteers in the congregation. She was committed to preaching ninety hours per month. My sister, with her severe social phobia, rarely went out preaching door to door. When she did, she was either with my mother or father, and she never did any of the talking. My sister was not likely to be a full time volunteer, so when my mother started crying that she wanted just ONE of her girls to pioneer with her, I realized the weight of that expectation was resting solely on my shoulders. I told her I would leave school and preach with her. To this day, that decision is one of my greatest regrets. Nevertheless, having made the decision, I let go of the dream of another degree, and I started studying for my board exams.

At the end of my Physical Therapy program, while I was doing my final internship, I met Kyle. Kyle was a boy one year older than me from a neighboring congregation. He played guitar in a friend's band. He was tall, and goofy. He also had a bit of an Afro, which was impressive for a white boy, and a pinky ring that made me question whether a Jehovah's Witness could have ties to the mafia. I was immediately drawn to his sense of humor. I liked that he was quick witted and made everything more fun. Within a few months of meeting, Kyle and I started formally dating, which is a big step in the Witness community. Dating in the cult was never casual, and more often than not, couples who start dating ended up getting married. Very quickly, I was head over heels for Kyle. In contrast to the way I grew up, where I was the mediator, and often made jokes in order to lighten the mood, with Kyle I could sit back and relax, and enjoy watching him be the center of attention. He made life more fun. After dating for a year, shortly after my twenty-first birthday, Kyle and I got married. Just before our wedding, I purchased a five hundred square foot, low income condo in Bedminster, New Jersey. Kyle was going to school to be a Nuclear Medicine Technician and working a paper route in the mornings to help him pay for school. I was working three jobs to pay the other bills. During the day, I worked in Outpatient Physical Therapy at the local Hospital, at night I worked as a bartender, and on weekends I taught Infant Massage classes. Still, as busy as we were, we were so happy together. The early years of our marriage were some of the happiest years of my life, and they made staying in the cult bearable.

In the first year of our marriage, I did a rotation in Acute care at a major trauma center in New Jersey. While I was working there, I was often asked to check in on patients who had refused to participate in Physical Therapy. I loved to sit and chat with these patients, determine their reason for refusing, and come up with a compromise that would help them achieve the goals they needed to reach in order to be discharged, while still acknowledging their reasons for hesitation. One of these patients was a woman who had just had an above the knee amputation. She had refused therapy because she was afraid of losing her balance now that she only had one limb. She was about five feet tall and at least two hundred and fifty pounds. She didn't trust that her remaining limb could support her weight. I sat next to her on her hospital bed and pulled the walker close. I promised her that I would not let her fall, that she was stronger than she thought, and that together, we could do this. All we needed to accomplish for that day was for her to complete a sit to stand motion, using the walker, five times in a row. She agreed to give it a try. After a solid pep talk, and my reiterating that I would not let her fall several times, she began to stand from the bed by putting her weight on her remaining limb and the walker. She was doing a fantastic job, but after the third repetition, I saw something in her body language shift. Her facial expression went from one of resigned determination to abject fear. She went pale and began to sweat. She was in a standing position, and I was standing in front of her with the walker in between us. As her fear overtook reason and she began to panic, she threw herself

47

backwards onto the bed, but the force of her body plummeting backwards shoved the bed backward enough that she was going to land on the floor. In that instant I remembered my promise that I would not let her fall, and so I threw my body forward, grabbed onto the gait belt around her waist, and held her up as I screamed for the nurses on the floor to come and help. My five foot ten body, leaning forward and holding up two hundred and fifty pounds of patient, was not sustainable, but I would not break my promise. As the nurses rushed in to help, I felt a searing pain in my spine and down my right leg. It was as if I had been shot in the lower back. I did not yet know that as my disc ruptured, the hot lighting bolt of nerve pain going down my leg would be my constant companion in the months to come.

I immediately stopped working and was put on Workers Compensation which meant that the Hospital would pay me 80 percent of my salary until I got well enough to return to work. Very quickly, I found out that the cost of keeping my promise to that patient, instead of lowering her safely to the floor as I had been trained to do, was two herniated discs in my spine. The pain was unbearable, and the fear of being out of work when I was still supporting Kyle through school was even more uncomfortable than the pain. I felt like a hypocrite. I worked with people with back pain every day, and I told them that I could help them feel better, and yet nothing I did was helping me relieve my own pain. I did all of the exercises and stretches I knew. I completed training and got certified as a Pilates instructor so that my core could be as strong as possible. I got my body fat down to eight percent. Yet, despite doing everything I knew to do to alleviate pain from a herniated disc, I was still having burning pain down my leg day after day.

One day, I was going through the mail and saw a flyer for "Fascial Pelvis" a John Barnes Myofascial Release class being taught about a half hour from my house in Princeton, New Jersey. I knew nothing about John Barnes, or Myofascial Release Therapy, but looking at that flyer, I got chills from head to toe. I don't know how to describe that feeling other than it was an inner knowing that somehow this course about the Pelvis could help my back. I had to take continuing education credits each year to maintain my license, and this course counted, so I had nothing to lose.

The day I showed up to this class, there was no man named John Barnes. There was a woman, a very small woman, who they called Mighty Mouse, teaching the class. She looked like the strongest woman I had ever seen, and I found out later that she was a women's champion in Taekwondo. She seemed confident, and full of life, and I immediately liked her. Over the course of the next three days, as she taught us several techniques to release the connective tissue, I felt my own body coming back to life. At the end of the third day, I was sitting in the audience and realized that my leg didn't hurt. It was then that I realized that the people performing these techniques were brand new to it. They were still learning how to perform these techniques, just like I was, and yet, even these basic techniques, performed by people who had no idea what they were doing, had left me pain free for the first time in years. I knew that I had to learn as much as I possibly could about this technique.

The week after the class, the instructor called me to follow up on how I was feeling. I told her that I had been completely pain free for a few days after the class, and then the pain had slowly returned. She encouraged me to go to John's clinic in

Malvern Pennsylvania for an "Intensive". During an Intensive, you would get three to four hours of treatment per day for one to two weeks. These treatments, in rapid succession, would create the biggest release in the facial system. It was thousands of dollars. By then, Kyle was working, and with a dual income, he encouraged me to do what I had to do to heal. I could only manage four days away, but I was able to schedule twelve treatments during those four days. It was also the first time I met John Barnes and was treated by him. After those four days, I was completely pain free and lost two pants sizes worth of scar tissue from my abdominal scar. I felt like a completely different person. I felt strong, and like I could stand up straight for the first time in years. I felt like I had experienced a miracle, and there was nothing I wanted more than to perform this miracle for others.

Over the next several years, I took every class that John Barnes offered, traveling from state to state to get the next credential. This technique not only changed the way I practiced physical therapy, and how I worked with patients, but it also opened my eyes to the fact that the body and the mind are more connected than I had been taught in my traditional Physical Therapy training. The mind/body connection was (and is) a huge hole in the standard medical treatment plan.

The biggest revelation for me was that you can not separate the mind from the body. Our connective tissue, also called the fascia, is one key to healing that I had never fully understood. In my Physical Therapy program, we had to dissect muscles of several different mammals in order to understand how everything comes together. We would encounter the fascia, this stringy white sheet of tissue, and the teacher would give it no more attention than to say "just cut through that to see the inside of the muscle." Occasionally, this fascia would also run through the muscle, and in between the muscle fibers. Again, we were instructed to ignore it, other than to cut through it. It wasn't until these classes in Myofascial Release, that I learned what a disservice that instruction had been to everyone taking this advanced science class in order to enter the medical field. The first issue with ignoring the fascia is that we were only ever exposed to the connective tissue of a dead animal. We didn't get to see what the fascia looks like in a living, breathing being. The second, and much more important issue was that we were never told that this tissue held the connection between the mind and the body.

As I continued to complete certifications as a Myofascial Release Therapist, I began to understand that this tissue weaves through our bodies like a spider web, and surrounds every part of our physical structures, even down to a cellular level. I was given the experience of seeing a video of the fascia releasing in a living human being. It was so beautiful! A restriction in the connective tissue would begin looking like a hard blob of grayish concrete, but as it released, and stretched back into a pliable three dimensional web, it would begin to glow and sparkle. It would shine like a body of water, when the sun is dancing along its surface. I was enthralled by how this tissue "came to life" as it was released.

In my training, fellow therapists who had received these connective tissue releases would experience waves of emotion, as if they were currently in the midst of experiencing a trauma. Many times there would be crying or screaming coming from the people around me, and then, after the release... a calm. You could feel each person receiving treatment shift from a stoic, competent therapist, to someone reliving an injury so intense that they had to bury it deep within their connective tissue to go on living. After that restriction was freed, you could visibly watch them morph into someone with the peace of closure. You could literally watch them heal, right before your eyes. It was like watching someone emerge from a therapy session where they were able to make a deep revelation, except with Myofascial Release, you rewatched the trauma happen, and then watched them survive it. They were exhausted, and tear stricken, but with the glow of someone who had finally let go of a deep pain they had been carrying around for years. Even though the trauma is held within the connective tissue, often a person isn't even aware that they were carrying this burden until it has been released. These traumas were often being held on a subconscious level, but the freedom from them was just as much, if not more significant. They had been fighting a battle they didn't even know existed. Once that subconscious battle was won by releasing the fascial restrictions, symptoms like fatigue, body aches, poor posture, nerve pain, anxiety, etc. would vanish. I couldn't help but think of the scriptures that talked about people healing by touching Jesus. Could he have been using Myofascial Release? Could this modality that incorporated energy medicine with physical touch be considered a miraculous healing? However it worked, I was all in.

As I laid on the massage table, allowing a fellow therapist to practice a fascial release technique, I found that no matter where on my body they were working, I would feel a deep pull, and burning sensation in the surgical scar on my abdomen. I made the profound realization that the belief systems I was experiencing during that time of childhood illness were buried in my surgical scar, and in the organs that had been damaged over these several years of infection. Emotions, whether pleasant or unpleasant, are experienced in the body as a chemical reaction. The brain sends the chemicals to our bodies and we feel whatever emotion is triggered. When there is too much of a particular emotion, whether it be sadness, fear, anxiety, pain, etc, the facia traps that chemical within it. The fascia changes from a more liquid gelatinous type substance, to a hardened chunk of connective tissue that physically encapsulates the chemical so that we are not overcome by that emotion. The trauma is literally entombed within us, to keep it stored away until we get to a point where our bodies are able to process and release it safely. The fascia of my body hardened to protect me from the overwhelming feelings of self hatred and abandonment by my Mother, and by God himself.

As a child, after the surgery, the fresh abdominal scar healed while sending roots of scar tissue to climb the fascia like ivy on a lattice. The abdominal scar tissue weaved itself within my hardened fascia, burying my feelings of fear, self loathing, and shame deep within my stomach so that I could carry on living without having to process these emotions. Once that connective tissue was released, I would experience waves of all of these emotions that had been trapped within me. The tissue would not release until the mind/body felt like it was safe enough to handle the healing process. You have to feel to heal. Once I felt safe enough to release these emotions, and a Myofascial Therapist provided the sustained pressure over that restriction, something called a piezoelectric response happened. It is a fancy way of saying, if a patient has the right mindset, and their body is ready, the therapist can use a low load of pressure, over a long period of time, to melt that connective tissue restriction back into a more fluid structure. The patient will experience the emotions that have been trapped as if they are happening in that very moment. If they are willing to fully feel them, the tissue will release and the patient will heal. If they are not ready to heal, the tissue re-hardens over that emotion so they do not have to feel it yet. It is the body's way of protecting the brain and the brain's way of protecting the body from going into shock. It is one big system that can not be separated out to treat the two sides independently. Having experienced this profound healing myself, I could not wait to begin treating patients and freeing them from their own traumas buried deep within their fascia.

CHAPTER 8

Jehovah's Witnesses make their money from member donations, so there is a constant push to baptize more people, to increase the amount of people donating. They do this under the guise that we are saving these people from destruction at Armageddon and giving them eternal life in paradise. For someone like me, who survived by being the ultimate people pleaser, I did everything I could to bring more people "into the fold". My purpose was to save lives, and my entire identity was wrapped up in being a full time minister or "pioneer". As a woman, I was never allowed to give weekly sermons, or hold any position of authority in the congregation, but I was allowed to preach by going door to door, and offering free home bible studies in order to convert more members. If I was in the presence of any male, and wanted to do anything that could be construed as teaching, I had to wear a head covering, like a scarf or hat, to remind myself, and everyone present, that I was submissive to the male members of the cult. It was a visual reminder that women were a second class citizen in the eyes of God. It also kept us humble when we dared to have an original thought. This misogynistic belief system added another layer to my negative self image that still continued to grow stronger day by day for as long as I was part of the cult.

At some point, the witnesses realized that Chinese people who were living in America liked to learn about Christianity in order to understand the main religion of the country to which they had immigrated. Under guidance from the "faithful and discreet slave", otherwise known as eight old white men who told the entire religion of seven million people what to do, the elders asked for volunteers to learn Mandarin so that we could preach to the Chinese community and convert more members. Again, in my eagerness to show my worth, and to make people happy, I convinced Kyle that we should volunteer to learn Mandarin, and join the newly formed Chinese congregation. Little did I know that this decision would play a huge role in my ability to leave the cult. Firstly, a cult can only maintain its hold on its members with a constant barrage of information. Mind control only works by feeding someone a steady stream of what you want them to believe, accompanied by a consequence so great that they are afraid to stray from that steady supply of information. When we started attending the Chinese congregation, I could no longer understand the sermons being given three times per week. This break in mind control gave me the opening I needed to begin to think independently, and question what I had been taught for my entire life up to that point. At the same time, I was spending day after day translating the literature the society printed and distributed, from Mandarin back to English. This was how I began to teach myself Mandarin. I would use the Jehovah's Witness publications, such as their religious books and magazines, published in Pinyin. Pinyin is basically the Chinese words spelled out in letters from the English alphabet so that English speakers can sound out the Chinese words. Then I would look up each word in a Mandarin to English dictionary, translate it, and write the

English word above it. This method resulted in a slow and painful process that took hours of each day to complete, but slowly we began to recognize certain words that were used over and over again.

Eventually, Kyle and I hired a private tutor to help us improve our use of the grammar and tones involved in the language. Over a period of months, I started to realize that when you translate a document from one language to another, you can't translate it word for word, because there are words in each language that do not have an equivalent in the other language. So, in order to translate something, you have to focus on the entire thought to translate the spirit of the message. With this realization, I began to think about how the Bible had been translated from God to man, and then from either Greek or Hebrew, to the English bible I had been studying my whole life. I realized that in those translations, individual words could be lost, and so we needed to place more importance on the spirit of the message rather than taking each verse word by word. Jehovah's Witnesses follow their translation of the Bible very literally. Word for word. For instance, their beliefs on not taking blood transfusions, or on shunning anyone who is not heterosexual are based on a literal translation of the words. These brief statements, supposedly spoken by servants of God, but translated numerous times, and never reiterated by Jesus himself, are responsible for so much hurt, and so many deaths within their organization.

I began to think about all of the scriptures that, when read individually, created these hard and fast rules that we were expected to live by. I started to picture millions of Jehovah's Witnesses as Amelia Bedelia, that girl from the children's novels who was told to "steal home plate" or "draw the drapes" and makes a complete idiot of herself by taking each word literally, and completely missing the point of the assignment. Then I thought about Jesus himself. He was a chill guy who hung out with the prostitutes and sinners. He didn't care what religion you were, he just healed you without asking questions. He knew there were rules about the Sabbath, but his followers were hungry, so he gave them grain and turned water into wine. I couldn't reconcile this image of such a loving and accepting man, with someone who would tell us to shun our families because they were born gay, or allow someone who needed a blood transfusion to die because a book written thousands of years before the technology to save lives with blood transfusions existed, said to abstain from them.

With this realization, I re-read the Bible, not focusing on each admonition word for word, but on the spirit of the message in the entire book that was "inspired of God ". With this reevaluation, my entire understanding of the Bible shifted. I realized that the ultimate message in the Bible is that God is Love, and so anything that does not support that proclamation can not be true. A God of love, who knew the forming of us even before we are born, would never create someone to love another human of the same sex, and then sentence them to death for following that love, for creating the emotion that is the very epitome of God himself. A God of Love would not sentence someone to a fiery death at Armageddon for receiving a life saving medical intervention. Most importantly, a God of Love would not torture us with shunning our families over "mistakes" that would be covered by his grace.

At the same time that Kyle and I began attending the Chinese congregation, I started a new job working at an Outpatient Physical Therapy clinic in Perth Amboy, New Jersey where almost every patient was Spanish speaking. I loved everything about this job. I loved that it was an extremely laid back environment. We could all wear jeans, and all of the employees ate lunch together. It felt like a family. I quickly fell in love with the Spanish culture and how warm and loving the people were. Where the Chinese congregation felt cold and distant, my work family embraced me in a way I had never experienced before. As I began to let my guard down and my true self shine at work, my married boss began to flirt with me. As much as I loved Kyle, that part of myself that was validated with male attention again rose to the surface. My boss was over a decade older than me, but very handsome, and I started to crave his advances. Just as I began to trust him, he started to ask questions about what it was like to be a Jehovah's Witness. Finally, one day, he asked me if there was anything I didn't like about being one of Jehovah's Witnesses. As I had been taught over and over again, I needed to be a good representative of the religion. I needed to honor God's name with my example. So, I answered "no." But this one question, so innocent and simple, stuck with me. It played over and over again in the back of my mind over the next several weeks. Each time the question resurfaced, I thought of another answer, a truer answer, that yes... There were things that bothered me about the religion. I hated that people who didn't follow all of the rules were shunned. I hated the religion's stance on homosexuality as a sin. I hated that women were not allowed to hold positions of authority in the congregation, and that they had to be submissive in any relationship. I hated the requirement of preaching door to door. And I absolutely hated the way the elders held judicial committees and judged the members for their sins instead of letting each of us speak directly with God. I also hated that Jehovah was often portrayed as a God of destruction and judgment rather than a God of love, grace, mercy and forgiveness. Each of these answers built a stronger wall around my heart until finally, a few weeks after the initial question was asked, I realized that there was no way this was the true religion. After finally beginning to let my walls down, and letting people at work see the real me, it became impossible for me to put them back up in order to pretend to believe something I didn't anymore. I needed to leave the witnesses. Over these same few weeks, my boss began flirting more and more, and I started to become addicted to the extra attention he was giving me. I needed a life raft, a group of people that cared about me, if I was going to leave the religion and be shunned. The thought of being shunned terrified me, but it also felt like a form of relief, knowing that I would no longer be responsible for holding my family together or for pretending to believe what I had been trained to believe for my entire life.

At the end of work one evening, while we were walking down the stairs, my boss said "what would happen if I kissed you?" Without waiting for an answer, he leaned over, gently pushed my back against the wall and kissed me. To say that I had mixed emotions was a complete understatement. The greatest emotion was guilt, that just like what happened with Steven, I had brought this upon myself for flirting with him and letting him think that I was interested in any kind of physical relationship. I also felt fear that if I rejected this man, I would make my work life uncomfortable, and this was a job I would desperately need if I was going to leave the witnesses and be responsible for my own financial situation. I also felt like rejecting my boss would poke a hole in the life raft of support I needed in order to move forward free from the cult. The first time I saw Kyle after this happened, I could not live with myself or the guilt of having betrayed him. I knew that I loved Kyle, but I also knew, without a shadow of a doubt that I had to leave the witnesses. I also knew that if I stayed married to Kyle, he would convince me to come back to the witnesses. Out of sheer confusion, one day while Kyle was at work, I packed up all of my things and left. I found a small studio apartment on craigslist not too far from the Jersey shore, and I moved in to try to clear my head, and try life on my own in a world I didn't know or trust.

Although I immediately felt a freedom like I had never known, I was also full of guilt and regret. I still loved my husband a great deal, but I knew that we wanted completely different lives. I also had my mother calling me every day, leaving messages in tears about how I had to come back to Jehovah. I felt like I was torn in two. I didn't sleep, I barely ate, and when I wasn't working, I would just put on my sneakers and run. I literally ran away from the cult. Within a month, I realized that as much as I wanted to be free from the Witnesses, I couldn't live without Kyle. I couldn't live with hurting him, when I loved him so completely. I went home, told him what had happened with my boss, agreed to leave my job, and he agreed to try to forgive me for allowing my boss to kiss me, IF we met with the elders. So again, I found myself in a back room of the Kingdom Hall of Jehovah's Witnesses, in front of a committee of elders, sharing my sins. This time my husband was sitting next to me. Again, the elders decided that no punishment was necessary, and that I could go on being a member of the congregation. As

61

soon as I resumed attending meetings of Jehovah's Witnesses, I fell into a deep depression. I couldn't live as a part of this religion, but I also couldn't live without Kyle.

I don't know much about astrology, but I do know that I am a double Aries. I have been told that being an Aries means we feel very passionately about things and that we have to follow our passions, or die trying. While I was still married to Kyle, who I was very much in love with, I knew that I would not be able to overcome this depression of pretending to be a Jehovah's Witnesses unless I found something else that I could really believe in. I was still taking classes in Myofascial Release therapy and I loved everything I was learning. I started using this technique with patients and they were seeing amazing results. Because I worked in an outpatient setting, I was seeing several patients at a time, and only had a few minutes of one-on-one time to do manual therapy with each patient. Still, even with this limited treatment, patients were calling into the office and moving all of their appointments over to my schedule, because they felt so much better after the manual treatment. My new boss, Mark, was a wonderful, humble Physical Therapist who knew so much more than I did, but saw the benefits my patients were getting from Myofascial Release. He agreed to give me more one-on-one time with patients. I started seeing one patient every half an hour instead of two or three patients an hour simultaneously. The results were unbelievable. Patient after patient was getting complete relief from chronic pain. It felt like a miracle.

Seeing these results, and craving even more one-on-one time with each patient, I decided that it was time to open my own practice. Kyle said I had his full support as long as I was bringing in the same income so that we could cover our bills. So, I continued to work for Mark in the outpatient physical therapy setting, rented a small room in a local plaza, and began seeing clients of my own on nights and weekends. Within three weeks I was making more at my own practice than I was making working for Mark, so I gave my notice, and set out to build my own healing center.

Because the witnesses are encouraged to support other members in the congregation, and because almost everyone I knew and hung out with were witnesses, most of the patients in my new practice were witnesses. Even though I loved my new practice, and was constantly amazed by what Myofascial Release could do, I felt like I had to censor what I said to my patients in case anyone was offended by the idea of "energy medicine". I had to be very careful not to bring attention to myself as a healer, because the idea of looking to mankind for healing instead of the Jehovah could be considered a "cause for stumbling". So with this level of censorship, I still felt like I was living in a world where I didn't belong. As I continued to treat myself with Myofascial Release, I started releasing harmful belief systems within my own connective tissue, and discovering my own truths that now made it even harder to attend meetings and listen to things I didn't believe. The depression creeped in around a feeling of being trapped. I could have my husband, or I could be true to myself. I wasn't ready to leave Kyle. I loved him too much.

As I was questioning everything about my life, I also began to question my sexuality. The first time I thought I might be bisexual was when I saw a movie with Scarlett Johansson. I was so drawn to everything about her, the way she looked, the way she talked, even how she moved. I told myself that I wasn't attracted to her, that I just wanted to be more like her. But then I met another sister in the congregation. She was my age and a biracial dancer. She joked that she and her husband both had a crush on me. I knew, without a doubt, that I also had a crush on her. But, because we were both married, and homosexuality of any kind is forbidden in the cult, that was the end of it. At least, I thought it was. But after Kyle and I split up the first time, and I came back, we were invited to go on a couples trip to Vermont.

There were four couples, including the dancer that had me questioning my sexuality. One night, the boys were doing something on their own, and so the four of us ladies decided to go in the hot tub. After many drinks, and spending a long time in the water, we decided to play truth or dare. At this time, the other three women in the hot tub with me were considered Pioneers, or the most devout members of the congregation. I, on the other hand, was just coming back to a religion I did not believe in, in order to keep my husband. I was not going to be the one to reel these women in, if they wanted to do things that were not technically "allowed" in the Jehovah's Witness handbook. Very quickly the game changed from truth or dare, to just dare, and the only dare was to make out with each other. So after a couple of hours of drinking, and hot tubbing, and daring each other to kiss, we all agreed that what happens in the hot tub, stays in the hot tub, and we got out, to go to bed with our husbands.

When I woke up the next morning, I knew I would have to tell Kyle what happened. Having just worked through a separation with Kyle, and not wanting to risk anything that could break his trust in me again, I told him what had happened the night before. He had a completely different reaction to the news that I had made out with other girls, than he did when I told him that my boss had kissed me. It was the same action, and yet, this time, because it was girls kissing, he just laughed it off. Unfortunately, one of the other husbands found out and did not take as kindly to the events that had occurred. He brought the issue up to the congregation elders, and again, I was involved in a judicial committee. However, this time, the Elders had no idea how to handle it. Apparently there is no chapter in the rule book for how to discipline sisters who get together and make out in a hot tub. Because the Elders did not know how to handle the situation, they wrote a letter to the Governing Body of Elders, or the top ranking Elders in the entire organization. This letter, explaining in detail our night of debauchery, was to be reviewed by these men who had a direct line to Jehovah. These men are charged with taking messages from God himself, and using them to guide and direct the entire organization. And now they had to take a break from communing with the divine to read about some girl on girl first base action. A few weeks later we got word that the Governing Body did not think any judicial actions had to be taken against us, but that all of the women involved would be stripped of their title as Pioneers. The announcement was made from the stage, in front of the entire congregation, that these women were being removed from their positions as full time volunteers and examples to the congregation due to their immoral actions. That was the end of it.

The way this situation was handled, by my husband and the Elders, added to the shame of not belonging. The events that happened were basically laughed off, like these feelings and actions weren't real or important because it was all between women. Again I got the message that being bisexual wasn't a big deal, or even real. So I told myself that I didn't have anything to worry about, or explore.

I was beginning to understand that I was indeed, bisexual, but it didn't seem to fully register, because it didn't change anything. I was married to a man I loved, and I had chosen him as my life partner. I knew that I had always wanted to be a mother, so I convinced myself that if I had a child, I could focus my attention on that baby, I could stay married to Kyle, and just devote all of my attention to raising that child, and drown out any other religious obligations. Maybe, if the religion was just on in the background, like tv static, I could be happy. Kyle agreed to have a child, but only if we stayed happily married, as members of the cult, for a full year. So again, I put on my happy face, pretended to be a believer that had repented of her sins, and carried on loving my husband. Just as the end of the year approached, I asked Kyle again if he would have a baby with me. He agreed, and after one night of trying, I got pregnant. I was over the moon.

CHAPTER 9

I was five days past my due date, out to dinner with my parents and my Aunt and Uncle, when I started having contractions. I decided it would be awhile before I could eat again, so I ordered dessert and then we headed home to try to get some sleep before the big event. I quickly learned that you can not sleep through labor, even if it is your first baby, and around two in the morning, we headed to the hospital. Labor was long, and not progressing as quickly as they wanted me to, so the Doctor decided to give me Pitocin to help make the contractions more productive. From that point on, labor intensified and by two pm, it was time to push. Kate was bound and determined to enter this world, and during the second push, she tore all the way through me, and came out guns blazing. I remember hearing Kate screaming, the look of concern on Kyle's face as he went pale, and the Doctor screaming "She's a Jehovah's Witness, there's too much blood!"

Jehovah's Witnesses believe that anyone who accepts a blood transfusion must be shunned, since Acts 15:29 gives explicit instructions to "abstain from blood." The Bible also says we should poop six feet from our house and then cover it up, but they don't take that one literally. I digress...

So, I am lying in a hospital bed, listening to the cries of my newborn baby girl, who I have never even held yet, realizing that if I pass out, my husband is going to refuse to give me a blood transfusion, and I could die for a religion that I don't even believe in. It was at this moment that I decided that no matter how much I loved my husband, I could no longer pretend to be a believer. Fortunately, my Doctor worked quickly, and after 27 stitches I was able to hold my baby girl, and eventually recover without a blood transfusion. But regardless of the outcome, a hard line had been drawn in the sand. Life was going to look different from here on out. Unfortunately, this new awareness, this new truth that I now understood with unquestionable certainty, left me broken hearted.

Kate had severe colic and cried for the first four months of her life. She also had blood in her diaper. I tried everything to remedy the situation. Since she was nursing, I eliminated any food that could have been an allergen from my diet, and yet she continued to scream. As difficult as this was, and as many tears as I cried trying to comfort my baby girl, it did provide a wonderful excuse to miss the three times per week meetings of Jehovah's Witnesses. Still, I would have done anything to make Kate feel better.

One of the sisters in the congregation heard about my plight with Kate and suggested I take her to visit a sister in New York a few hours north of us. Apparently this sister had trained in a technique called Bioenergetic Kinesiology and could use your muscle to test what was out of whack in the body. She had been brought in before the elders many times to determine if her talents were a link to Satan himself, but they had never been able to find fault with her. I was intrigued. I had learned about Kinesiology in school for Physical Therapy, but I had never been exposed to using the muscle as a way to determine what was going on throughout the body. I drove Kate the two hours to see this woman. She screamed the entire drive, and when I pulled up to the address I had been given, I was distraught to see that this woman was working out of a run down trailer in the middle of nowhere. Still, we had come this far, so I grabbed Kate and went in.

This sister held various objects up to Kate's stomach and tested them with her own muscle to see which ones made the muscle weaker and which ones made them stronger. She stripped Kate down naked and placed her onesie on her belly, then she tapped a series of acupuncture points and removed the onesie. She muttered a few more questions under her breath and Kate's countenance visibly changed. Kate signed a deep sigh, and fell asleep. This woman declared that Kate was allergic to cotton, or more specifically, to the pesticides they use on cotton, so every time we put her in a cotton onesie or diaper, or blanket, she would scream bloody murder. Apparently what this woman had done was to hold acupuncture points in the presence of the allergen to retrain the body not to shut down those meridians in the presence of the substance. It felt like magic. It felt forbidden, and yet a sister was performing the technique. I knew that if I could learn this technique, and combine it with Myofascial Release, the healing that would result would be nothing short of a miracle.

I drove home with an entirely different child. Kate cooed, and laughed, and slept the entire drive home. Over the next few months, our baby girl grew, gained weight, and became the happy baby we had always imagined. I also sought out classes to learn this life changing technique so that I could add it to my bag of healing tricks with my own patients.

Around this time, I realized that my get out of jail free pass from having Kate was about to expire, and that I would have to explain to Kyle why I wasn't going back to meetings at the Kingdom Hall. The pain of even thinking about this conversation and what it would mean for our future was too much to bear. I numbed my mind by playing on the floor with Kate and watching television, by eating mindlessly, and by trying to pretend like this reality wasn't fast approaching. Finally, I couldn't put off telling Kyle that I wanted out of the cult. To my surprise, when I brought it up, he said he knew. He said he could see me fading away again, and that he could tell that I was unhappy. I asked Kyle to move away, and start over somewhere new, where we could stay married and I wouldn't be the evil person who had left the religion. Kyle said that he wasn't willing to leave all of his friends, and his family that had supported him when I left the year before. So my options were to stay in a marriage where none of our friends could speak to me any longer since I would be shunned, to be alone three nights per week, and watch my husband cry as he walked out the door to meetings of Jehovah's Witnesses without me, to always feel guilty that I was the evildoer in the eyes of everyone we knew...or to leave my marriage. This time for good. The choice was not easy, it was the hardest decision of my life. This decision meant missing out on half of Kate's childhood, and leaving a man I was still madly in love with. Still, it was the only way I could see Kyle or myself having any chance at a happy future. It was also the only way to expose Kate to a life outside of the cult.

I faced the reality that I was about to be a single mother with an infant and nowhere to live. So I thought about the only person I knew who had left the cult and might be willing to help me. I thought of Justin VanDusen, that fourteen year old boy who had broken my heart over a decade before. I had heard through the grapevine that he had left the cult to pursue a music career, and he had been shunned. This is when I learned about a new social media platform called Facebook that might be able to help me get back in touch with Justin. After a quick search, I found Justin and sent him a message letting him know that I was getting ready to leave the cult, and that I didn't know anyone on the outside that might be able to help me with this transition. I did have some family outside of the cult, but I didn't want to put them in the middle of myself and my parents, so I knew I had to reach out to someone unrelated, with no connection to my parents.

In our first conversation, I asked Justin how he was since he had left the cult. He responded that he was now a quadriplegic. He had been celebrating a record deal when he dove from a hotel balcony into what he thought was the deep end of a pool below. It turned out that he dove, head first, into the shallow end and suffered a spinal cord injury that left him paralyzed from the neck down. Since I had gone to school for Physical Therapy, and had a background in caring for people with spinal cord injuries, it seemed like the universe was offering me an olive branch. It just so happened that Justin was looking for someone to take care of him over the night shift. Medicare would pay me to watch him overnight, while both of us mostly slept. I could bring Kate with me, and she could sleep in the portable crib, I could sleep on the couch, and wake up when Justin needed something. Then I could still work doing Physical Therapy during the day, on the days

71

when Kate was with her father. It was a plan that allowed me to make enough money to support myself without losing time with Kate. If I was the statue inside the marble, Justin gave me the chisel to start breaking myself free.

So when Kate was nine months old, I left the house Kyle and I shared, all of our earthly possessions, took Kate with me, and got an apartment a half an hour away to start over. I could not answer phone calls from any friends or family because I knew that they would be urging me to return to the cult. It was as if everyone I knew died on the same day. There was no one who understood what I was going through except for Justin.

Over the next few weeks, I kept myself too busy to grieve. On the days that I had Kate, I spent time with her, and we took care of Justin together. When she was with her Dad, I tried to figure out how to rebuild a practice that went from being successful, to losing ninety percent of its patients overnight since those patients were Jehovah's Witnesses and could no longer come to me for treatment now that I was labeled "bad association" as an unbeliever.

I took any free time I had and submerged myself in the world of information I hadn't been allowed to read or learn because it was part of "worldly" knowledge we were told to keep clean from. When you leave a cult that has told you exactly what to think, feel, and do for your entire life, the ability to make your own decisions and create your own moral compass feels extremely overwhelming. I decided I would read as much as I could about as many religions as I could, and whatever the common denominators were in those religions would become my new belief system. What I discovered in my study of Christianity, Buddhism, Judism and Sufism is that all things in life boil down to love or fear. Some religions call it good and evil, or light and dark, but in the end every decision boils down to choosing love or fear. With this new paradigm of "choosing love" I knew that whether the question was "How am I going to rebirth myself into this foreign world?" Or "How am I going to support myself and my daughter without a support system?" Myofascial Release was the answer.

I found a Holistic Physical Therapy practice less than a half an hour away from Justin's house that specialized in Myofascial Release Therapy. It was owned by a man who often taught John's seminars and had the nickname "the Prince of MFR". I knew that I could learn a lot from this man, and that I could grow professionally by being associated with his practice. I reached out to him, and by some sort of divine intervention, he was hiring. I went to meet him for an interview, and in my traumatic state, I told this stranger my entire story. I told him that I had just left a cult, was a single mother, and that I needed a safe place to start over. I remember looking at this man across the table of the Italian restaurant where we had met for our interview. He sat in silence, slowly stirring his soup, and processing this dumpster full of information I had just spewed into his lap. He looked up and asked me "Are you any good at Myofascial Release?" I replied "That is about the only thing I am sure of right now." After lunch, he had me demonstrate my technique on him, and within a few hours, I was hired.

At this practice, I met so many people who accepted me for exactly who I was, unconditionally. It was a new kind of family, and it was the first time that I realized I could belong to another group. I could be authentically me, and still have friends, and be included, and celebrated as someone with value. I worked alongside a Buddhist Myofascial Release Therapist whose wife was battling terminal cancer. He practiced with joy, and grace, and I immediately felt comforted by his presence. I met a "mama bear" therapist who brought me boxes of plates and cups that she no longer needed. They were the first possessions I was able to call my own, after leaving everything I had behind. They were all solid white and I remember thinking they were a perfect representation of my "clean slate" moving forward. Most importantly, I met my Erika.

Erika was a young girl right out of high school. She had just started college, and was working as a receptionist at the practice. She was loud, and inappropriate, and full of love and energy, and she was wonderful. As I began to rebuild my career, and struggled to balance child care and work, Erika offered to watch Kate so that I could work more hours and make enough money to get my own place. When I told her I wanted a tattoo so that I could have a visual reminder that I no longer followed the rules of the cult, she booked us an appointment and got a tattoo with me. She was my ride or die, and my first real friend outside of the cult.

As time went on, Justin began to make some improvements under my care. He gained some range of motion with regular Myofascial Release treatments, and he seemed more excited to pursue ways that he could return to computer work with adaptive equipment. At the same time, he also began to show more of his true colors. He would have someone hold a cigarette to his lips so that he could smoke. He drank excessively by having someone put alcohol in his cup. He said he needed to continue to do these things so that he could feel like the guy he was before his accident. I started to worry about having Kate around Justin and his friends when they were drinking and smoking. One of Justin's caregivers would steal his pain medication and was often passed out in the living room. As much as I understood Justin's desire to remind himself of the life he used to have before the accident, I questioned whether living with Justin was a good environment for Kate, as she was getting older and absorbing more of the world around her. Justin also began to make it clear that he wanted more of a romantic relationship with me. Although I was so grateful for our living arrangement, and I loved him deeply, I began to feel like I was trapped in another situation that wasn't allowing me to grow and develop my own safe place for Kate.

Through Justin, I was able to reconnect with other Jehovah's Witnesses that I had known as a teenager who had left the cult. It felt wonderful to find a new community of people who understood what it was like to be alienated from everyone you knew, and more importantly, what it was like to try to live your truth on your own. Unfortunately, the majority of people who have the means and strength to leave the cult are men, so as I reconnected with this group of men who had left, I often struggled with maintaining the lines of friendship. Not wanting to lose any more connections, I often allowed these relationships to become unhealthy, and progress to physical relationships, which made me feel dirty and reignited my feelings of worthlessness. I also learned that not everyone willing to take you into their circle is worthy of trust.

I learned that the safest thing to do was to throw myself into work, so while I worked three days per week in New

York learning from the "prince of MFR" and his crew, I also resigned myself to start building clients back up at my own practice in New Jersey. Before long, I had more patients than I could handle, and I was consistently blown away by the healing my clients would see with the combination of Myofascial Release and Bioenergetic Kinesiology, especially in patients who had survived unspeakable trauma.

CHAPTER 10

O ne day a man entered my practice in New Jersey. He was a veteran who had fought in the Gulf war. His wife had made the appointment, and he was hesitant that I could help him with the chronic pain he had been experiencing since he was thrown from his vehicle during a roadside bombing in Iraq. As I began to work with him, he got very quiet. He was lying face down on the table, and I was working on the connective tissue in his low back, performing a lumbo-sacral decompression, when a smell filled the room that I had never smelled before. I broke the silence and asked him if he could smell that smell. He said yes. I said "what is it?" He said "it's burning flesh". He had been in a tank in Iraq that hit a mine and exploded. He was thrown from the tank, while the rest of the men in his platoon were bombed to death. The impact of him being thrown from the tank caused a serious back injury, but as it's meant to do, the connective tissue hardened in order to protect his spine. While hardening from a liquid to a concrete substance, the fascia trapped the chemicals that surrounded him, the smoke, the burning flesh, the bomb, and the terror. Now that he was safe, and we were working to release the fascial restrictions in his lower back to ease his pain, the connective tissue got the message that it was okay to liquify. As the tissue released, those substances that had been trapped in his body were released from his body, too. He had literally been carrying around his dead comrades for years. This man never returned to my office because the treatment "freaked him out," but his wife reported that his physical pain subsided to a much more manageable level, even after only one treatment. This experience changed me as a practitioner, and as a person suffering from chronic pain. I began to really believe that emotions are held within our physical body and must be released in order for us to heal completely. Trauma of any sort, emotional or physical, literally changes the shape and make up of our physical form.

Any time you are living a life that doesn't align with your core values as a human, you are creating stress and disease. Stress comes from emotions like fear, dread, anger, frustration, sadness, grief and anxiety. My husband is an executive for a fortune 200 company. His boss once told me that "Pressure is constant, but stress is self-induced." I couldn't agree more. Two people can have the same experience but perceive it differently. This perception dictates our body's reaction to the experience. So much of our negative emotions, and our body's physical response to those emotions, results from the way we choose to look at our circumstances. For the things we can not change, we need to figure out how we can look at them differently. But from my personal experience, there are not many things that we truly can't change.

As I continued working with patients with chronic pain, I saw more and more people who had been living while physically embodying massive traumas.I fully believe that God, or the Universe, or whatever name you choose to call a higher power or vibration, puts opportunities for us to heal in our path, over and over again, until we finally get the lesson. In my case, more and more patients started coming in that were healing their trauma from sexual abuse. I had been ignoring the signs that it was time to heal the physical and emotional wounds around my own sexual trauma with Steven. But one patient changed all of that. Her name was Sarah and she was a professional dancer. I immediately felt a connection to Sarah. She was a Mormon, and I felt like I understood the thought process, and physical guarding that comes along with being a part of a religious cult. She came in with hip pain, but she would physically pass out any time we did any work on her pelvis. After a few weeks Sarah called me on my cell phone. I was driving home from work, and I remember hearing the fear in her voice. She was crying and terrified, and I knew she needed help but was so afraid to ask for what she needed. I pulled over to the side of the road so that I could give her my full attention. During that conversation, she confided in me that she had been suffering extreme physical and sexual trauma at the hands of her biological Father for several years. I told her I would do whatever I could to keep her safe and that we would find a way to stop this from happening together.

Years later, Sarah confided in me that it wasn't until our conversation that she ever allowed herself to believe that she could get free from this abuse or that it could ever end. As I struggled to find support systems for Sarah that could help her hide from her Father and protect herself, my phone rang with a New York City number. It was Sarah. She had been attacked by her Father again, she was in the emergency room, and she was very badly hurt. I grabbed the first train back from Jersey into New York City and raced to be with her in the Emergency Room. The nurse, who had been trained in treating rape victims, sat down to do the rape kit while I held Sarah's hand. She lifted the sheet to examine Sarah's wounds, and immediately passed out. The violence of the attack, and the resulting physical damage was more than she could physically handle. I spent the next two days with Sarah on the run from her Father. We stayed with my friends in New York, that her Father wouldn't know, as I tried with renewed determination to get her the protection she needed. In the end, Sarah was able to move to another state where her family could not find her, and she began to undergo several years of surgeries to fix the hip trauma from her years of sexual assault. Today she has become a therapist that works with other people to overcome their own traumas.

After living through this experience with Sarah, I decided that I needed to become certified as a Women's Health Therapist. I was not prepared for the wave of trauma that would arise in my own body as I completed that certification. The training with John Barnes was designed to release all of the connective tissue restrictions in the pelvic floor. Each therapist was partnered up with another therapist so that we could practice these techniques on each other. These techniques required internal manipulation of the fascia. I wish I could explain the sounds of trauma releasing that filled the room as we learned each technique: a room full of women, whose fascia was holding on to years of sexual abuse and trauma. With each technique, each release of pelvic floor fascia, there was weeping, screaming and shaking. These women were healing, but it was devastating to feel the vibration of pain that these women had been holding onto for so long. This work felt equally terrifying and important. Once I completed my certification, I went back to work ready to embrace a new clientele of women who desperately needed my help.

CHAPTER 11

O nce word of my training got out, I was receiving more referrals than ever to work with women both in New York City and in my office in New Jersey. The sheer amount of women with pelvic floor issues as a result of trauma, astounded me. It felt like the phone never stopped ringing, and I was so grateful to be able to be with these women as their fascial restrictions released, and they let go of tremendous pain.

In one session with a young woman who was seeing me for chronic abdominal pain, I got ready to perform some internal vaginal releases. As I lifted the sheet to access her vagina, I saw something strange. This girl had a razor blade inserted into her vagina. She was a young woman in her early twenties who had moved back in with her parents after college to save money. Her mother had inserted the razor blade into her vagina as a punishment for spending too much on her credit card. The girl cried and told me I couldn't remove the razor blade because then her mother would know that I knew what happened. That was not an option. I removed the razor blade, and did energy work around the area to help her start to heal from the trauma without irritating the tissue further. Again, I started the urgent and stressful process of helping a woman escape to another state, so that she would be safe from the sexual torment of a parent.

Another young woman named Erin came in with her mother. She had been training with the Olympic development program with a goal of joining the United States Olympic Field Hockey team. On a break from her training, she was walking across the street and was hit by a car. Her injuries were so severe that her dreams of playing Field Hockey professionally vanished. For years she had been suffering with chronic migraines, dizziness, nausea, and pain. As we began working together, her physical symptoms began to resolve and in the coming months we built a trusting relationship. She was getting stronger and healthier, but something was still holding her back. In one session, she confided in me that her ex-boyfriend had raped her several times. We began some external Myofascial Release to her pelvis, and as her connective tissue released, she also released the emotional trauma of these attacks. In the end, Erin realized that she was a lesbian, and that much of the emotion she was still holding in her connective tissue was a deep seated fear that she was not lovable and would never find someone to love her for her authentic self. As her fascia released, and we continued working together, Erin was able to understand that she was so worthy of love. Today, she is in a long term, healthy, committed relationship with her lovely girlfriend.

Another woman named June began seeing me because she could only walk short distances without extreme fatigue. She had severe body aches and muscle pain, and required a scooter to get around and 24/7 nursing care to help her with her activities of daily living. June came to see me several times a week for years. We worked on releasing her connective tissue in a way that made her feel safe and seen. By the time we finished our sessions, June had come to the realization that her emotionally abusive husband was contributing to her physical aches and pains. Having released all of the traumas she was holding in her connective tissue over their many years of marriage, June was able to make the decision to leave her husband. Shortly after asking her husband to move out, June was able to sell her scooter, walk independently, decrease the amount of assistance she needed at home, and most importantly to her quality of life, she was able to return to driving.

With all of these patients, the symptoms were physical, the treatment was physical, but the healing was emotional, spiritual, mental AND physical. The fascia is what ties it all together. It protects us when we are unable to deal with what is currently going on in our lives. It encapsulates the trauma and holds it safely in our bodies until we are ready to process it. We can cope with a certain amount of fascial tightness before we experience pain. The body is extremely good at compensating for these restrictions, but eventually you will hit the final restriction that the body can't adjust around. This is when we start to experience pain. This is why it is so important to continue maintaining treatment or a home program to keep our fascia loose, because by the time your body tells you that there is a problem, there are already layers upon layers of restriction that are impeding your body's ability to take care of itself. These restrictions make our body work harder to accomplish basic tasks like sitting or walking. Tight fascia can affect our bodies down to a cellular level, impeding the cells from eliminating toxins and keeping the body dehydrated. The energy meridians that are strengthened with acupuncture flow through the connective tissue, so tight fascia can also disrupt energy flow to all of the organs and systems in our body. In the case of these women who were healing from sexual assault, the chemical reactions created by their trauma, kept tight in the tissue, were telling their subconscious that the trauma was still happening, playing it on a repeating loop over and over again in their subconscious as they went on with their daily lives.

Time and time again, these women showed up on my table. Women who needed to escape, to get away from the people who were supposed to love them but were instead causing them immeasurable pain. I knew that the Universe was leading these women to me because I myself had escaped an impossible situation when I left the cult. I also understood what it felt like to have sexual shame as a result of trauma. I was their safe place, the person they could confide in, but with each patient that I helped, my heart would break a little more. I struggled with the realization of how many women walk around in unbelievable fear and pain. My empathic side was feeling their pain as if it was my own. My fight or flight reflexes kicked in on their behalf, and my cortisol levels skyrocketed. My mentor in Myofascial Release has said that you can only take someone as far in their healing as you have gone in your own healing. My mentor in Bioenergetic Kinesiology calls it "tripping over your own work." You have to heal your own body, mind, and spirit, before you can treat others. Otherwise, if you help others before you have helped yourself, your own body will suffer for it. This is exactly what happened. I knew I was needed, and I wouldn't abandon these girls, but I felt thoroughly out of control and unable to protect them. So I controlled what I could, and went back to my old faithful coping strategy. I stopped eating.

Obviously, I didn't stop eating entirely, but I liked the feeling of control as I cut out entire food groups like sugar and grains, and watched my body get smaller and smaller. Shortly after moving out on my own, I was diagnosed with Attention Deficit Disorder, and that diagnosis came with medication that diminished my appetite, and made it even easier to cut my calories. I lived off of coffee and stimulant medication with an occasional salad or bowl of roasted veggies. Most days I was eating no more than five hundred calories. This way of eating served three purposes. One, it allowed me to shrink down to a size that society felt was appropriate for someone in the field of Physical Therapy. Two, it cut down on food expenses as a single mother, and three, it made me feel like I could control something when the world around me was less certain. I was a single mother running a business with varied income, but I could count on the number on the scale to go down when I wanted it to. I was able to hide this behavior from my family and friends because even eating limited calories for years, my body was still at the high end of what is considered a "normal" weight. In fact, with each visit to the Doctor to check up on the stimulant meds, she would praise me for losing weight. I was anorexic but still in a body that was borderline "overweight". I convinced myself that if the Doctor said I was healthy, then my disordered eating must not be a real issue.

Around this time, I took Kate out to breakfast at a local diner. As we were getting ready to leave, I saw a familiar face in one of the booths. It was Jacob, the kid with the orgasmic pen from seventh grade Spanish class. He was wearing the same oversized hoodie and baggy jeans and he still carried himself like he did whatever he wanted, whenever he wanted to. I said a quick hello as I walked past him, and the friends he was eating with, and I went home with Kate. Later that day I had a Facebook message from Jacob saying that it was nice to see me, and that Kate was adorable. It was just after Christmas, and Kate was going to be with her Dad for several days, so Jacob and I made plans to meet up for a drink at a local Irish pub. I got there first and sat down in a booth. Jacob showed up soon after and asked what I wanted to drink. I told him I would have a Guinness. He gave me a slightly impressed smirk and went off to the bar. He came back with two pints of Guinness and we started to talk. He was exactly the same guy I remembered. He was handsome, witty, and a ball buster. He had become kind of a big deal in the music industry, and he was working with some of the great Jazz musicians that my father had always admired.

Several people in my family, on both sides, are musicians. I was raised with a reverence for the arts, and for music. One of my favorite memories was singing with my Dad's Jazz band at a club in Montclair, New Jersey called Trumpets. I was immediately drawn in by Jacob's explanation that he did what he did because he loved the idea that he was commemorating a point in time: that song, at that time, in that place, would never happen again. He was documenting a moment in music history. And of course he was a musician himself. How could he have grown up to be anything else? The Jacob I knew could never grow up and work a 9-5 job somewhere. This artsy side of him was so intriguing. It took that one night, that one date, to reignite that crush I had on Jacob years ago. Jacob and I dated, off and on, for nine months after that. I was so in love with him. He made me relax. He taught me that life didn't have to be so serious all of the time. He helped me let go of a little bit of control, and he inspired me to picture a life where Kate and I could have someone come home to us again.

Jacob and I didn't have a problem loving each other. I don't want to say that part came easily, because nothing about our relationship felt easy, but it was powerful, and wonderful, and I would have done anything to make him happy. Unfortunately, due to my history, I really struggled with anxious attachment. I needed constant reassurance that Jacob did love me, and wasn't planning on leaving, and he was not the type of guy to be held down. In the end, I sabotaged the relationship by trying to get stability and security from a man who was meant to be free. The very thing that attracted me to him was what made me pull away. I chose fear over love and our relationship fell apart.

In those nine months that Jacob and I dated, I pulled farther and farther away from Justin. Although I would always be thankful for Justin for how he had helped Kate and I break free from the cult, it was too hard for me to watch Justin continue to drink and smoke and refuse to take care of himself. I didn't want Kate to be around someone who was making those choices, and so I created space between us. Regardless of how much I tried to pull away, Justin always reassured me that he loved both Kate and I, and that we would always be important to him.

Justin had taken out a lawsuit against the hotel where he suffered his spinal cord injury. Although he was the one who jumped from a balcony into the shallow end of the pool, the pool had not been maintained. The water in the pool was cloudy which was what led to the confusion about which side of the pool he was jumping into. The pool also had no signs saying that it was closed or off limits to people staying at the hotel. In the end, a judge ruled that Justin was 49 percent at fault, and the hotel was 51 percent at fault. Justin was awarded millions of dollars for his injury.

At the same time, the house that Kyle and I had bought when we were married had dropped in value significantly. After we bought the house, there was a massive flood that affected most of the town we lived in. Although our house never flooded, the downtown area was deserted due to water damage, and gangs moved in. Three young men were shot execution style around the corner from our house, and houses all around us were in foreclosure due to the crash in the housing market. By the time we wanted to sell, we owed more than one hundred thousand dollars more than the house was worth. The only way out was to foreclose on the house, or declare bankruptcy. I had also allowed my business landlord to use my credit card for thirteen thousand dollars of repairs on the building where my office was located. He told me he was renovating a new space for the business and that he would purchase the business, pay off the credit card, and hire me on as a salaried employee when the renovations were done. I desperately wanted the stability that came with a steady paycheck and health benefits, so I agreed. In the end, the landlord bailed out of the deal and left me holding the bill for the repairs on his building. With these two things looming over my head, I called Justin to ask him what I should do. He said "You have a millionaire who loves you more than anything, and will always take care of you. You can declare bankruptcy and start over. I will always have your back if you need it." So that's what I did. I declared bankruptcy, knowing that if I ever needed to take out a loan, Justin would co-sign.

As I was going through my bankruptcy, and my break up with Jacob, Justin called and sounded very depressed. He said he was struggling with living life as a quadriplegic and he needed to find some kind of purpose again. I reminded him that his purpose in this life, what made him feel alive, was to make music. Someone with a C4 complete spinal cord injury, like Justin, should not have been able to breathe on his own, but he could, because his neck muscles were so strong from singing with the band that they were able to lift his rib cage. I encouraged Justin to spend some time at a rehab where they could help him strengthen his voice so he could get to a place where he could sing again. Shortly after his stay at Kessler to rehab his voice, Justin passed away in his sleep. They believe that his muscles gave out from overuse. I still carry this guilt with me, that maybe my suggestion, and the resulting therapy contributed to his death. In the end, I know that Justin's spirit was too big for this world. I know that this is not the first lifetime we have spent together, and it certainly won't be the last. Still, at that time, I felt like not only had I lost my best friend, but I had also lost my safety net. I had also lost the only person in the world who loved me unconditionally. That loss alone made me question my own worth again. Now it was just me and Kate, with no back up plan. I had never felt so alone.

CHAPTER 12

As we finalized our divorce, and Kyle moved on and got married, I decided that I needed to take a solo trip and get to know myself better. When Justin died, I was 29 years old. I had hung up a map of the United States. I remember thinking "If I die tomorrow, there would be so many places I would die without seeing." This thought made me set the goal to see all fifty states by the time I turned forty. Justin and I had planned to go on a trip through the western states to explore what this country had to offer. He died before we were able to go, but I decided that I needed to go on that trip anyway. There was a continuing education class called Myofascial Release for horses, in Longmont, Colorado so knowing I could write off the trip as a business expense, I decided it was a sign to move forward. I booked the class, and made arrangements to crash on a friend's couch for a few days while I was there.

On the first day of class, I rolled up to a ranch in the middle of nowhere. There were several horses, and I was surrounded by "horse people". I'm not sure if I have given an accurate description of where I grew up in Morristown, New Jersey, but we were a suburb of New York City. We had projects and yes, there were some more rural areas, but I had never been anywhere near a horse. The size of the horses immediately intimidated me, and when I wasn't completely afraid of being trampled to death, I was put off by the smell. It turns out that horses often pass gas when they are treated with Myofascial Release. It also turns out that flies love when horses pass gas. So I made it through one full day of the class, and then decided that this was decidedly NOT a service I would be adding to my practice. So with no hotels booked, and no plans other than to hit the open road, I took off the next morning from Colorado to New Mexico in search of adventure.

I can't remember if it was on my way to Taos, or on my drive from Taos to Utah that I encountered a long stretch of road with nothing at all around me. I remember looking at the gas gauge and wondering if I had enough to get me to the next area of civilization. I also remember that the road was beginning to get dark, and I had not seen any other cars for quite some time. In a fit of panic, I pulled over to the side of the road and got out of the car. I started kicking the dirt and screaming that this was all Justin's fault... that he was meant to be with me, and I shouldn't have to do another thing all alone. As I was hitting the crescendo of my massive tantrum, hundreds of hot air balloons came up over the mountain range in front of me. Instantly, I knew two things. One, that civilization was just over the next mountain peak, and two, that I wasn't really alone. I sat and watched the balloons float up into the sunset, gathered my strength, and got on with my drive.

At the end of that trip, I wanted to fit in one more hike before I had to head back to Colorado to catch my flight home. On my last night, I walked into the dive bar next to my hotel and asked some of the locals where I could do a quick hike in the morning. They recommended a hike called something like "Dead man walking" but assured me that it was quick, easy, and beautiful. The next morning, I rode out to the trail, and didn't even bring water with me, thinking it would be a quick excursion. I took pleasure in the red rock dirt on my shoes, and the relatively easy climb. But before I knew it, I was wading through a stream and climbing up a mountain ridge with a rather steep drop beside me. At one point, the trail got so treacherous that I sat down on my butt and started scooting along the path with my legs dangling off the side of the mountain. Again, fear overtook me, and I decided to sit still and regroup. Once I quieted my mind, I heard people's voices above me and realized that one way or another, I had gotten completely off the trail.

It was a simple mistake that resulted in a profound understanding. I realized how many times in my life I had kept pushing to hit a goal or to achieve the next milestone, without ever stopping to check in with myself and see if I was still on the right path. That moment still comes back to me often. The feel of the dirt, the panic flowing through my veins, and my determination to finish even though it felt impossible. It turns out that sometimes things feel impossible, because they are not the path we are meant to travel. Also, just because something is easier, that doesn't mean it isn't beautiful. I made my way back to the trail and came across two older women who looked at me like I was a rabid animal climbing out from the bushes. One woman handed me an extra water bottle and with equal parts compassion and disapproval on her face said "oh honey" as they moved past me to descend the trail. Now hydrated, and once again on the right track, I finished the climb and was rewarded with the most beautiful rock formations I had ever seen. I sat in silence, and gratitude for that hiking trail that taught me that it's okay to "let it be easy".

During the year that Justin passed, we rented a little yellow house. I loved that house. It was old, and drafty, and poorly maintained, but it had a little yard, and a room for Kate and I, and a tiny little porch where we could sit and watch the world go by. A few months after we moved in, a hurricane hit New Jersey with rain like we had not seen in years. The rain was pouring through the roof into every room of the house. I had more leaks than buckets, and eventually fell asleep in Kate's bed because it was the only part of the house that didn't have rain pouring through the ceiling.

A few months later, I started to notice that I was feeling short of breath when I would go for my walks around our hilly neighborhood. Kate also developed a cough that wouldn't go away. Her doctor said that it was a "nervous tic" and not to worry about it. So I didn't worry, until one day I was moving things around in Kate's closet and I noticed that the walls in the back of the closet were covered in black mold. Her closet shared a wall with my closet, and to my horror, the mold had started climbing up my closet walls as well. The landlord was mortified, and quickly moved Kate and I into an apartment in the next town. So all at once I was grieving the loss of my little yellow house, of Justin, of my relationship with Jacob, of the bankruptcy, and of our health. It felt like we had hit rock bottom.

Having hit rock bottom, I learned that someone, even in the most powerless situation, can take their power back. Nothing is ever permanent. No situation, financial status, job, or problem is forever. We get to choose the life we will live.

Sometimes that choice isn't easy, and it will require a period of "death" to everyone around us but through letting those situations die, we are free to be reborn. One way in which I toyed with rebirth was with the continual questioning of my sexuality. Now that I was free of the cult, and free to make my own choices, I again considered the idea of dating girls. There was a bartender at the bar around the corner from my apartment that I was extremely attracted to. She was older than me, and she had a seriousness about her. I was just attracted to her energy, her whole vibe. I was told that she wasn't into women, so I never said or did anything about it. But again, this questioning of my sexuality kept nagging at the corners of my mind.

Around the time that Kate turned four or five, she started telling me that she was a boy, and wanted to be called PJ (her initials) instead of Kate. She always wanted to wear pants, and refused to wear anything "girly" let alone a dress. Unfortunately, when she attended the meetings of Jehovah's Witnesses, she was required to wear a dress. Kyle and I went to mediation about this issue, and he was told that making her wear clothing that was not in alignment with her gender identity could be very damaging. He was not supposed to force her to wear dresses to the meetings. He stated that this was disrespectful to the organization and their rules. The Mediator wrote into our agreement that Kate would dress formally (suits or dress pants) to show respect for the religious setting, but that she could not be forced to wear a dress. Despite Kyle's agreement with this stance during mediation, Kate was continually told that she had to wear a dress to meetings. I had several photos of her in the dresses she was forced to wear to the meetings, but never pursued things legally, because Kate didn't want to upset her father.

While all of this was going on, I still had very limited contact with my parents. But I felt moved to reach out and tell my parents what was going on, and how I felt the religion's stance on homosexuality was harming my kid. My mother responded by saying "Why are you labeling Kate with something that you aren't even sure she is, when the result of her being that thing could be destruction at Armageddon?" At the same time, the Jehovah's Witnesses organization put out a video where they show kids how they should approach people with same sex parents. In the video, they tell children that they should tell people in homosexual relationships that Jehovah doesn't like what they are doing, and that they need to change their actions or be destroyed by God forever. Up until this point, I had never officially left the witnesses. I just "faded", which means that I didn't respond to communication from the elders. This would leave me still listed among one of their members, but I would be considered "inactive". After this video, I knew that I wanted nothing to do with an organization that held these damaging beliefs. So I wrote this letter formally disassociating myself from the Christian Congregation of Jehovah's Witnesses:

May 26, 2017

To Whom It May Concern,

Although I have not attended the meetings of Jehovah's Witnesses in over nine years, I did not feel the need to write my letter of disassociation from the organization until now. I hesitated to write this letter because I did not want any negative impact on my parents. However, in light of the recent video regarding Jehovah's Witnesses' stance on homosexuality, I feel that it is extremely important to make it clear that I am not longer a part of this organization. I do not agree with the organization's stance that homosexuality is a sin. I still have a very close relationship with Jehovah God, and through his guidance and direction, I have come to the understanding that, above all else, God is love. It is impossible for him to be anything other than love. When I was a pioneer in the Chinese congregation, I learned that, quite often, when translating text from one language to another, there is not an exact translation. Instead, you have two get across the spirit of the message. Although I respect the Bible as a sacred book, I believe that in translation, some of the texts were misinterpreted. As a result of this understanding, I now consider the spirit of the entire book. I focus on God's whole message, rather than reading it one verse at a time. We must love our neighbor as ourselves. I do not feel that there is any circumstance in which a God who knows us, even in the womb, would hold the way we are created against us. Nor would he prohibit the experience of love. I know that Jehovah can read my heart, and he knows that I am good. I am made in his image, and therefore I am inherently enough. I have learned that when we choose fear over love, we crowd out love, which is the personification of Jehovah himself. Instead, I choose to live each day choosing love over fear. My God is not one of retribution or punishment, but one of grace, compassion, and unconditional love. I strive each day to embody these characteristics as well. That being said, it is with a heart full of love that I formally disassociate myself from the Christian Congregation of Jehovah's Witnesses and the Watchtower Organization. I do not wish to be contacted over this decision.

Love and Light,

Megan Bingman (Formerly Megan Jensen)

After I emailed this letter to the headquarters of Jehovah's Witnesses, my parents reached out and said that they were so ashamed of me. My mother said that she was devastated that I would let this "one ideal" prevent me from being a member of the true worshippers. As she said those words, I realized that it wasn't about "one ideal". It was about my identity. Of course I had always fought this belief, because it was the right thing to do, but in that conversation I realized that I was fighting for myself. I was asking my parents to choose me, their bisexual daughter, over their religion, and again, I wasn't being chosen. I never will be. The depth of that hurt, of that rejection, is so deep that I can't even put it into words. I know that I am not alone in this experience either. There are thousands of Jehovah's Witnesses who have come out as members of the LGBTQ community, and who have suffered the same, if not worse, rejection than I did. And there are hundreds of thousands of people around the world, who are not Jehovah's Witnesses, who have been rejected by their families for the same reason. It is for this reason that my life's purpose is to help people be their most authentic selves, and to support them in whatever they need to make that possible. My mission, in this lifetime, is to remind people that they are so much more than enough, exactly as they are.

Another one of my most important re-births came at the end of my worst relationship. I had been briefly dating a man I met online. He was a single father, and was not scared away by the fact that I had a daughter. Within a few weeks, he had asked me to move in, but I knew this decision affected Kate as well as myself, so I told him I wasn't ready. In the next few weeks his true colors began to show. He would get extremely angry, and refuse to talk to me, if I would hang out with any male friends. The final straw was when I got sick with a bladder infection, and he was livid that I wouldn't continue to have sex with him while I was sick.

That experience was enough for me to decide that it was time to give up on dating altogether. This relationship fell apart in October, and left me feeling lonelier than ever. It was just before Justin's birthday, so I decided to go see a spiritual medium in order to speak to Justin and hold him accountable for leaving me. When I arrived at the medium's house, there was a live praying mantis just hanging out on her front door. I thought that couldn't possibly be real, but when the medium answered her door, she was just as shocked as I was at our visitor. She walked me upstairs into a beautiful sunny room in her home. She got quiet and asked Justin if he would like to join us. The first thing she said was "I see a mountain range, rising up out of red rocks. There are hundreds of hot air balloons. Justin wants you to know that he was there with you, that you were not alone, and that you are never alone now. He is always with you, and he is watching over your son."

I was simultaneously shocked at how this woman could have described my experience so accurately, but then how she could have mistaken Kate for my son, when she is clearly my daughter. Looking back at this moment, I wonder if the medium was picking up on Kate's gender fluidity, or if she was foreshadowing a son I would have in the future. With trepidation, I asked the medium if Justin knew if I would ever find someone who would love me unconditionally like he had loved me. He replied that I had already found the man I was meant to be with, but that I had written him off, and I needed to go back. That night, I went through my planner, reviewing all of the bad dates I'd had, growing ever more certain that none of these men were my soulmate. I decided that the message must have gotten lost in translation, and that the only sane thing to do was to give up on dating, focus on raising Kate, and follow my passion for healing people who could not afford to pay. In honor of Justin, I started the leg work of opening a non-profit foundation to provide Myofascial Release and Bioenergetic Kinesiology to patients who could not otherwise afford personalized medical care that would not be covered by insurance.

Within a few months, the JVD foundation was born, and I began raising money that I used to cover my expenses while I treated veterans suffering with PTSD, women with breast cancer whose insurance benefits had run out, and domestic abuse survivors. I knew what it was like to be left in the lurch, totally alone, and to wonder how my basic needs would be met. Justin knew that feeling too, and yet, through Justin I also learned that being there for someone at their lowest point is the ultimate display of love. Every time I put my hands on a client, I would first set the intention that this person left my table knowing that they were loved unconditionally. I wouldn't say it with words, but my goal, each and every day, was to wake up and make people feel seen, heard and cared for. In that exchange, something magical happened, I connected to a vibration that filled me up, and I began to help myself as much as I was helping others. Each day, I ended work by cleaning up my sheets, and packing up for the day. As I got ready to leave, I would quiet my mind and send out a vibration of gratitude...for work that allowed me to spend time with Kate and also support us, for each client that walked in my door, for my hands that were able to relieve the pain and suffering of others, and for the calm I felt wash over me as I worked. I ended each day in gratitude. Something in me began to shift. I had a glimmer of feeling worthy of all of the love and support that I gave to others. I asked the Universe to please surround me with people who would treat me the way I treated others. I needed people I could trust, who would love me unconditionally, like Justin had. I needed to know that he wasn't the only person who could ever love me like that.

After a little while, I decided that I would like to expand my non-profit to include working with people in other countries. The only person I knew who had ever worked on international missions was a guy I had gone on one date with, named Jim. We had connected through an online dating platform. We talked through emails and over the phone for weeks, and there seemed to be a spark, but our communication wasn't consistent. He would get busy and forget to reach out, or he would call from the car and I would cut the conversations short because I couldn't hear him over the road noise. Eventually, we set a time to meet for a date. He walked up to the table where I was sitting, and, although I recognized him from his pictures, his energy was not at all what I had expected. He was closed off, almost confrontational. He seemed irritated with me. Every time I would begin a sentence, or share a thought, he seemed to disagree. He also really seemed to love Jesus, and the Bible, and appeared turned off by my "spiritual, not religious" stance. At the end of our date, he gave me a quick hug and walked off. I wrote this one off as a loss. Yet, we had several friends in common that vouched for his character, and I knew that he had spent a lot of time in Haiti teaching the people there about sustainable agriculture.

So, on Thanksgiving day, 2012, I texted Jim and asked him if it would be possible to learn more about getting involved in the Haiti trips. I told him that I would like to offer Physical Therapy to people in need there. He suggested that we meet up for dinner and he could fill me in on all the details. So eight months after our first date, we met up again. When Jim walked into the restaurant this time his energy was completely different. His face lit up in a kind smile, and he started joking around almost instantly. He was a completely different person! He was open and receptive, and really seemed interested in hearing about why I wanted to do medical missions. Mid-way through dinner, Jim apologized for his behavior on our first date, and explained that he had been trying to quit smoking, and was on day two of a cold turkey approach when we first met. I have never smoked, but immediately I understood that the guy going through nicotine withdrawal on our date eight months prior was not the real Jim. After our second date, Jim and I were inseparable. By April we were engaged, and by June we were married. Somewhere along the way I remembered Justin's admonition that I had already met the man I was supposed to marry, and that I should go back. If I had any doubts at all that Justin had been referring to Jim, they disappeared when I found out that I was pregnant on Justin's birthday that year. I felt like he was giving me his blessing to start a family with this man I had just married.

CHAPTER 13

J im, Kate and I moved into a house in New Jersey on three acres of land, next to a horse farm. It was the epitome of peace and quiet. It also had a separate apartment downstairs where I could see patients. It gave me the ability to continue to work from home while raising our new little girl, Georgia. I was healing from twenty two weeks of bed rest with Georgia, and beginning to see patients again, when I started to feel a stirring in my soul that a big change was on the horizon. A friend of mine had recently married a licensed Psychiatrist who also gave tarot card readings. I decided it wouldn't hurt to see what he had to say about this feeling like things were about to change. The dichotomy of a licensed Psychiatrist incorporating spiritual practices into his work intrigued me, and so I paid out of pocket to hear what he had to say. He did my reading and said that the overwhelming theme of the reading was Death. As someone who had been taught that death without resurrection was the worst possible outcome for an unbeliever, I tensed at the word. He soon explained that death is not a bad thing. Death can mean the closing of a chapter, and the beginning of something else. The death of leaving the Witnesses and losing so many of my friends and family felt like a very literal death. I knew what he meant, that death could mean change, and with Jim as my new support system, I felt ready to tackle whatever would come our way.

Shortly after Georgia was born, I kept remembering the medium saying that Justin was looking after our son. We now had two daughters, and I could not physically go through another pregnancy, but I felt a call on my heart to be a foster parent. I brought it up with Jim, and his response was "I have always wanted to be a father. The ultimate gift would be to know fatherhood in all of it's forms. I would love to be a father, a step father and a foster father." He was all in. I started scrolling through the profiles in our local SWAN directory and saw a picture of an almost sixteen year old girl that was currently living in a group home. I emailed the social worker that was in charge of her placement, and found out that she was having physical issues as a result of trauma, and those medical needs were what prohibited many families from considering taking her on as a placement. As a Myofascial Release Therapist trained in women's health, I felt like this pairing was fate. So, Jim and I scheduled to start PRIDE training as a prerequisite to her being placed with us.

The social worker was not allowed to tell this child that she had a family that wanted to bring her home until we had finished the training, and were clear to take the placement. They didn't want to get her hopes up in case something came up. Unfortunately, as soon as she turned sixteen, she was legally able to sign herself out of foster care, and she did. She would never know that we were working so hard to bring her home and that she was already so loved and wanted. I can only compare that loss to a miscarriage. There is a child that is so wanted, and you have a plan to bring them into your home, you are doing all of the hard work to prepare, and then all of the sudden, the child is just gone. As I was just wrapping my head around this news, Jim told me that he was offered a promotion but we would have to relocate to Altoona, Pennsylvania. When I looked at a map, I saw that Altoona was only forty five minutes south of State College, Pennsylvania, where the main campus of Penn State University is located. My Grandfather had grown up in State College, and was a die hard Penn State fan. I took this as a sign that we should move. Maybe our third child was in Pennsylvania.

I can't share too much about our foster to adopt experience in Pennsylvania because it involves trauma that isn't just mine to tell. What I can say is that if your gut is telling you that something is wrong, listen to it. Shortly after moving to State College, we finished our training as foster parents and were matched with a nine year old boy who had been in six other foster homes. We were able to meet him in April, he started staying with us on weekends until school let out in June, and then he moved in. We were told, in no uncertain terms, that our son had never been a victim, or perpetrator, of sexual assault. We found out later that the social workers were aware of the fact that this was not true, but hid the information from us in order to make the placement.

After five months and one day of our son living with us, we were able to adopt him. We still had some reservations about his mental health, but we also knew that he was not going to get the help he needed while on Medicaid, and that the only way to really help this boy was to get him on our health insurance, so that we would have access to better doctors and therapists. Over the three years that he was with us, we loved him like our own. He was ours. We sat in court and affirmed it. Still, over those years, and especially as he entered puberty, it became apparent that he was Bipolar, and despite treatment and medicine, his impulsivity and mood were not well managed. We knew, before I was told for sure, that our adopted son was hurting our daughter. We have more than one biological daughter, and I will not name which child was involved. As much as I need to tell the story from my perspective, the story from her perspective is hers alone to tell. That being said, when I realized that something was wrong, I called his Therapist and asked her to investigate my instincts. Unfortunately, all she did was reiterate proper boundaries with him, and sent him back home. I'm not sure what else I was hoping she would do.

The day I found out for sure that he had been hurting my daughter was the day my life ended. To be clear, I obviously went on living, but I wished I didn't have to. I could feel that my soul, my life force, was no longer in my body. It was like when I went sky diving many years earlier. Right before I jumped out of the plane, I could feel my soul leave my body. It was as if I was watching myself jump, rather than experiencing the jump from inside myself. I understood that my awareness was leaving my body as a coping mechanism. Part of my training as a Myofascial Release Therapist included an explanation of what happens when we feel extreme trauma. Sometimes, it is too much for our body to process events as they occur, and so we separate from ourselves. It's almost like we are looking down at ourselves from above, because processing the trauma as if we are watching it happen to someone else is easier than processing the trauma ourselves. In terms of the sky dive, I felt my awareness re-enter my body as I was floating safely back to earth. I only needed that separation to jump out of the plane.

When we are talking about repeated trauma, like a child being abused or a victim being assaulted, that separation of awareness can last much longer because the body just doesn't have the resources to process it without going into shock. Many times in treatment, you can see the moment that the patient's awareness re-enters their body. The body becomes physically heavier, oftentimes there is a moment of stillness where the patient's body remains in the position of injury which the fascia releases, and the emotion is processed. Thisthis stillness is usually followed by an emotional release. The person who walks out of that treatment room is an entirely different person than the one who walked in. They are no longer in pieces. That's the beginning of healing. It's messy, and it's painful, but it's how our body gets from one side of the trauma to another.

The day my daughter told me what had been happening, we were driving home from the Emergency Room. I didn't want our son to overhear, so I asked Jim to meet us in the car. We sat in the car, in the garage, while she told Jim the same information she had just given me. Jim and I just started at each other for a moment. We reassured our daughter that she was not in trouble and that we would handle it, and keep her safe. I slept in her room that night, although there wasn't really any sleeping. There was eight hours of me staring at the ceiling, wondering how I could have let my baby girl get hurt. It was eight hours of the most extreme guilt, knowing that it was my actions that brought this child into our home. It was my fault that he had hurt her. I had been the parent who was home when he hurt her. I was in the kitchen, making dinner, completely oblivious to the fact that this terrible thing was happening in the finished basement directly below me. I am not sure I will ever forgive myself for that. I should have protected her. I should have known. And the truth is that some part of me DID know. I could feel it when I had the undeniable urge to put alarms in the hallway, so I would know if our son left his room at night. I could feel it when I would go check on the kids downstairs when things got too quiet. I could feel it when I would stand hidden around the corner and listen to him talking to her, desperate for him to admit to what I was sure had already happened. But every time my skin crawled, and my intuition screamed at me to do those things, the results came up empty. I would blame myself for not trusting him. I thought maybe I was projecting my own childhood trauma onto them. I thought "this kid has been through enough, why am I trying to ruin this placement for him too?" All along that feeling in the pit of my stomach was right. A mother knows, even when she wishes she doesn't.

The next morning we called Children and Youth Services, and the police. I needed someone else to tell me what to do. I have never seen the movie "Sophie's Choice" because I have never been able to handle sad movies, and yet here I was with my own Sophie's Choice right in front of me. I had to choose between my children. I had to choose who to protect, my son or my daughter. I had to choose whose life to destroy completely. In the end, there was only one choice to be made. Our son needed more help than we could give him, and he needed to be in a home without other children. I needed to protect my girls. Knowing that this was the right decision mentally, did not change the fact that losing a child broke my physical body. The day they took our son back into foster care, I started hemorrhaging blood so badly that I went to the Emergency Room. They ended up giving me four times the normal dose of birth control to try to stop the bleeding, but it didn't work. I was losing my child, and my uterus was quite literally weeping from the emotional pain. I also spiked extremely high blood pressure as a side effect of the stress and the very large birth control dose. After that day, we were not allowed to see our son because he was so desperate to come home, that they were afraid seeing us would give him false hope that that could ever happen. It was just like the day I left the cult. This person, my son, who I loved and who was a huge part of my world was just gone, without a trace. It didn't feel survivable.

Within a few weeks, I was scheduled for a hysterectomy, since the uncontrollable bleeding was causing severe anemia. My blood pressure was so high that they were not sure if doing a surgery was even safe, but the morning of the surgery, I squeaked in just under the maximum blood pressure allowed, and I was wheeled in to surgically remove my uterus. I was trying to save my life by cutting out my body's physical reaction to this unbelievable amount of stress. So in the middle of what should have been a time to grieve the loss of my child, I was in the hospital undergoing major surgery, and was completely overcome by my body's betrayal. Even being in unimaginable pain, in the middle of all of this physical and emotional chaos, I reverted to my old coping mechanisms and took it upon myself to act happy, and funny, and be a people pleaser. I literally wanted to die, but as they wheeled me into surgery, I noticed that a transport tech named Baby had been pushed against the wall by my gurney. The last words I said before I went unconscious from the sedation were "No one puts baby in the corner." The sound of the medical staff laughing as I slipped into unconsciousness felt like validation that I had again avoided my pain by keeping everyone around me happy.

During my hospital stay, I had one wonderful nurse who kept saying "if you have pain below the belt, call your doctor, if you have pain above the belt, go to the Emergency Room." I didn't fully comprehend what she was saying, but I remember that she repeated that admonition three or four times during her eight hour shift. I had been managing the pain well with Tylenol, but in the middle of the night, I requested another dose. The nurse said that I had hit the maximum allowable dose for Tylenol, but that the Doctor had also written for Demerol so I could try a dose of that if I needed it. A few seconds after administering the dose into my IV, the veins in my right arm became very dark, and appeared like they had all risen to the surface of my arm. In my altered state, I called the nurse and said "I think I'm turning into the hulk". Apparently the medicine had burned the veins from the inside out. She marked a Demerol allergy in my chart, and I went back to sleep without any further complications.

The day after my surgery, I was released to go home. I was home for less than a day when my right arm started aching. I thought back to the weird Demerol reaction and figured that, although my arm looked normal again, the pain in my arm must be the result of that allergy. Yet, in the back of my mind I kept hearing that nurse say "If you have pain above the belt, go to the Emergency Room." I had just learned, in the worst possible way, what happens when you ignore your intuition, so I told my husband I thought I should go back to the hospital just to be sure everything was okay. Lying in the Emergency Room the Doctor on call said "I think you are fine, but just to be sure we are going to do a CAT scan." I have truly terrible veins, and my arms were covered in bruises from failed attempts to place an IV. They had to call in a technician with a fancy X-ray type light that would light up and show her where my veins were. Finally, she was able to place the IV and I was transported to the CAT scan.

As I laid there I heard the technician say "This IV isn't good enough for contrast, we will have to put in another one." That was my breaking point. I started to cry and told her that I would just forgo the CAT scan and go home, that I was sure everything was fine. She said they would just try to use the IV that they had because any result, even if it wasn't perfect, was better than not doing the scan at all. After a quick scan, the technician came out and said "we got a very clear picture of what's going on." Her demeanor had changed from someone who was frustrated and overwhelmed by my lack of cooperation, to a look of pity. She even stroked my hair as I got settled back on the bed for transport. Right after I returned to my room, the Doctor sat down next to my Emergency Room bed and pulled up my images. "It's a Pulmonary Embolism. I wouldn't have guessed it. Good thing you came in." In that moment, some mysterious protocol was alerted, and the room filled with nurses and technicians all taking my vitals, and preparing medications. I was given a dose of Heparin, and admitted to the cardiac floor. Over the next twenty four hours I would learn that an untreated Pulmonary Embolism has a mortality rate of up to thirty percent, and one in ten patients with a pulmonary embolism die suddenly with death being their first and only symptom. If I had ignored my arm pain, or gone home without that CAT scan, there is a three out of ten chance that I would have died. In my case, it was called a "provoked" pulmonary embolism because they knew why it happened. Birth control, especially at the dosage I was taking, in combination with surgery, made me a prime candidate for a clot.

Although there was a physical reason that this embolism formed, I am also keenly aware that this pulmonary embolism was provoked by my wanting to die. I truly felt that I couldn't go on. As I healed simultaneously from my embolism, and my hysterectomy, I experienced a fatigue like I had never known. Yet even while feeling this extreme fatigue, and recovering from these life threatening ailments, two weeks after coming back home, I jumped back into my job as a Mom. I didn't want the girls to be experiencing the stress of a sick mother on top of losing their brother. My surgeon happened to be our next door neighbor. She had told me to expect six weeks of healing in bed, so when she saw me pulling up to drop the kids off at the bus stop two weeks after my surgery, and resulting Pulmonary Embolism, she questioned if I had given myself enough time to heal. I told her I was fine. And on a conscious level, I was. In order to go on living, I had completely left my body, and so whatever my body was experiencing, whether it be pain, or anxiety, or crippling fatigue, I was able to ignore it, because I wasn't connected to my physical body at all. This sounds great, and it allowed me to resume my parenting role, but it turns out that your physical body needs your energy to be within it, otherwise it starts to fall apart.

Despite our best efforts to return to a normal, healthy family, reminders of the loss of our son were everywhere. People in the neighborhood, and at the kid's school, would ask where he was. Worst of all, they would ask the girls where he was. The girls didn't need to be talking about our loss, and I got tired of seeing the looks of pity on other mother's faces as we walked through the neighborhood, or when I stopped by the school. The final straw was that our daughter refused to go into the basement where she had been hurt, because it made her feel anxious. So shortly after my surgery, while still recovering from my Pulmonary Embolism, my husband and I decided that we needed to move.

This decision was compounded by the notice we got in the mail that, although our son was adopted from the foster care system, and children and youth services were the ones who ultimately made the determination to move our son into a home without other children present, we were ordered to pay child support to the state for his care. The amount of child support ordered was almost as much as the mortgage on our home. So we decided to sell the house, and use most of the equity to pay down enough debt so that we could afford the child support payments.

Despite paying child support, we were only allowed to see our son one more time, several months after he was removed from our home. We met in the office of his Therapist. The tiny room was packed with his Therapist, a Social worker, our son, my husband, and myself. The purpose of the meeting was to tell our son that he would never come back to live with us again. As we all sat in a circle looking at each other, my husband tried to deliver the news to our son, but he broke down. The Therapist tried to tell him, but was unable to come up with the words. Finally, I looked my sweet boy in the face, and said "We forgive you for what you did, but our job is to keep all three of you safe, and we can't do that if you are all living in the same house, so you won't be able to come back and live with us again. You will have to stay at your current foster home now. The picture of my twelve year old son, sitting on that Therapist's couch, silent, as a tear rolled down his face will haunt me forever. He was born addicted to several drugs, and the part of his brain that is responsible for impulse control isn't and will never be, fully developed. This dichotomy of a sweet, funny, smart little boy whose bed was covered with stuffed animals, being the same person as this monster who violently assaulted my daughter, still haunts me. As my sweet boy cried, I stood up, gave him a hug, and told him that I would love him for the rest of my life. Then I turned my back on my son, and walked out of the room. I never saw him again.

We were asked not to have any contact with our son after that meeting because he was having trouble bonding with his new foster parents, and in truth, they needed him to forget us. We were able to send him a card on his birthday, but after that last birthday, we were no longer allowed to have any contact. In the midst of being separated from our son, we hired a lawyer to fight Children and Youth Services to make sure he was getting the care he deserved. He was not being medicated appropriately, he was not being given the therapy that he needed, and he was not getting the services he would need to succeed. So, while being completely shattered physically, emotionally, and mentally, we spent thousands of dollars we did not have on a lawyer to fight for our son's rights. It would be another year and a half, and a change of social worker, before our son would begin to receive the services we were fighting for. As part of that process, we had to terminate our parental rights, so that his current foster family could adopt him, and he could have the sense of permanence he needed to continue healing from our failed adoption. When you terminate rights to a child, you have to sit in front of a judge and say that you are okay with not knowing anything that will happen to your son in the future. You agree that you have no authority over this child, and that you are okay with life moving forward, as if he was never born. Agreeing to those statements shattered whatever was left of my broken spirit. My life force left my body. That's when my physical body literally started to break.

CHAPTER 14

In an effort to make the house feel less empty, we got a new puppy. This required taking the dogs out every few hours as we were house training them. Of course, we decided to do this in Pennsylvania, in the middle of the winter. The backyard could only be reached by going down a flight of stairs to a concrete stoop, and we had to have the dogs on a leash, because they could fit through the slats in the fence out back. On a particularly icy morning, as I was holding both dogs on their leashes, I turned to talk to my daughter behind me, and as the dogs ran forward, I lost my balance. They dragged me down the flight of stairs. I landed on each icy step, feeling my tailbone break, and then continue to bounce, broken, down the rest of the stairs.

Looking back, I know that at least part of the reason for my imbalance was because I was still out of my body. My awareness of where my body was in space was compromised because it was too painful for my soul to re-enter my body, so it just stayed away. I also think that immense amount of pain was the only way that the universe could direct my attention back to my neglected body. The pain was unbearable for weeks, but it also served a purpose. It gave me a reason not to work. At the time of this accident, I was still specializing in Women's Health, and so the majority of my patients were victims of sexual assault that were coming to heal their old wounds. I used to take pride in this patient population. I loved helping women heal, breaking through the barrier of trauma that had been stored in the connective tissue, and in many cases, improving the chances that a woman would be able to get pregnant. But once my daughter had been hurt, I could no longer handle this patient population. The universe was doing everything in its power to protect me from having to connect to the vibration of victimized women. So, my body broke, and it demanded my attention. For the next four weeks, I listened to what my body needed as it began to heal.

The first day that I was able to return to driving, I felt the financial pressure to return to work. So I put the healing that had begun over that month on the back burner, took off my patient hat, and put my therapist hat back on. I called one of my patients, told her that I felt well enough to treat again, and scheduled her next appointment. Within minutes, I walked around to the back yard with the dogs, and started to slip on the muddy hill. All I could think was "I will NOT fall on my tailbone!" Instinctively I protected my tailbone by pitching myself forward, landing on my outstretched left arm, and felt a pop. My hand stayed planted on the ground, as the rest of my body continued sliding down the hill. I saw stars, got nauseous, and felt like the wind was knocked out of me all at once. I screamed for my five year old to bring me my cell phone, which she did, and then hid under her bed because the sight of me lying on the ground crying with my arm in an unnatural position scared the living daylights out of her. I called my husband and said "I think I dislocated my arm. I might be able to pop it back in myself but I need to get my jacket off." The second I got the jacket off, I saw my bone protruding through the elbow in a way that let me know I would need more help than I could give myself. Two fractures and a torn ligament later, I was out of work again, before I had even had time to treat the one patient I scheduled.

By the time my arm healed, a virus called COVID-19 had begun spreading through China and there were whispers that cases were beginning to show up in the United States. Before I could even think about re-opening my practice, the world shut down. Quarantine would become an ally in the fact that I wasn't expected to return to work, and an enemy in that I had nothing to do but grieve and heal my wounds, but with the kids home all day every day, I was never alone for long enough to process my grief. As an Executive, Jim was also required to take a ten percent pay cut to help the company get through the pandemic. Financially, even after moving houses, we were barely staying afloat. With Jim's pay cut, the continued child support, legal expenses, medical bills, my inability to work, and a fixer upper home that needed endless repairs, we were broke. The financial stress, on top of everything else, felt like the final straw. By the end of August, the kids were getting ready to return to school in a hybrid model, with a few in person days, masked, and a few virtual days, learning from home. The day before school started I got a call from Jim who asked "are you sitting down?". He then told me that he had been offered a promotion that would alleviate our financial issues, but it would require a transfer to Maine, and if he takes it, we would be moving in two weeks. We couldn't afford to say no, so the chaos of an interstate move, during a pandemic, began.

When we arrived in Maine, Jim's company put us up in temporary housing. It was an off season lake house with one hundred and eighty degree views of the water. It was impossible not to fall into the rhythm of the lake. Despite the move, and the pandemic, sitting there on the porch, listening to the lake water hit the shores, I was able to take a moment and be still. My breath began to match the movement of the water. I would allow myself these moments of stillness, where I was so grateful for this ease of financial stress, and a safe, fresh start for my girls, but also where I could safely let the sadness break through me. That's exactly what it felt like. I had to let myself crack open. Those moments where grief poured out of me and seemingly, fell into the water, were life changing. The weight inside of me slowly lifted.

Still, there were plenty of things that continued to distract me from healing. I threw myself into getting the kids settled in school. I planned day trips to show the girls our new home, and decide what town we wanted to settle down in. Next, I hyper-focused on buying a house in an impossible market. We ended up finding a home in a neighborhood with new construction. Someone else had built the house, and then was not able to obtain financing, so this gorgeous home in our dream neighborhood was suddenly available. We moved in, and began to find our new normal.

Then, when everything was more settled and I was again left alone with my thoughts, I began to panic. The emotions seemed to come to the surface even when I didn't have time to process them. My older daughter was still doing online schooling, and I needed to keep it together for her, but holding in these emotions that desperately wanted to release made me feel extremely anxious.

The thing is that we can use anything as a distraction... it can be alcohol, food, exercise, reading, even binge watching television shows. Our minds are very good at distracting us from healing the emotions we do not feel we are ready to process. The only time we can really heal is in stillness. In Bioenergetic Kinesiology, we call it "rest phase". Our lives are broken up into work, play, rest and sleep. We need to keep these segments balanced in order for our state of health to improve. Most people do pretty well with work and play, and a little bit less well with sleep. In contrast to those three segments, most of us do not rest at all. Rest is when we are awake but sitting, or laying still, with no input or stimulation, no external sounds or information. Watching television or reading are considered play, but being still, only listening to the sounds of our breath going in and out, is considered our rest phase, and it is imperative to healing. This is why meditation is such a healing tool. It forces us to be still, and allow the things that need to heal to come to the surface.

I truly believe that in order for me to have the stillness that I needed to heal, the universe stepped in. In January of 2021, I contracted COVID. I was at high risk due to my asthma, and history of pulmonary embolism, and we were still learning about this virus and how to treat it. I had to quarantine from my family, so alone, in my bedroom, with nothing to distract me, I fell apart. I slept, and processed my grief. I rode the waves of fear that once again, I was facing something that could kill me. Over those ten days, something in me let go. There is something about being faced with a life or death situation that makes you question what is important. I could decide to stay trapped in this straight jacket of hardened fascia, or I could allow the emotions to surface and release. My best friend would send me messages of her singing a little ditty that became my mantra "Feel, Heal, and Grow. Surrender to the flow."

The Angel in the Marble

During that quarantine, I was healing from COVID but also from all of the events of the previous years. Emerging from that room gave me the opportunity to test out my new beliefs. For instance, was I ready to move on from a career that made up so much of my identity over the last fifteen years? I have built a reputation as a Myofascial Release Therapist. I am really good at it. I have spent years of my life and tens of thousands of dollars training in this technique. I make good money doing it. But, being still helped me accept the reality that it no longer feels right in my soul to practice it. Still, the universe tested my new understanding.

When we first moved to Maine, I was told by many people I respected that my skills were desperately needed in the area, and my husband and I were trying to cash flow an expensive and extensive home renovation. In the end, I let fear make the choice for me. I succumbed to the fear of not having enough money, of being afraid to try to find my true calling, fear of losing out on all of the praise and adoration I got as a Myofascial Release Therapist. I signed a year-long lease, and again, within two weeks I had more patients than I could handle. But this time, I woke up each day with a deep, dark, pit in my stomach, knowing that although I loved helping people, I was not on the right path.

I remembered the reading where I was faced with the "death" card. At that moment in time when I was closing my practice, and we were moving from New Jersey to Pennsylvania, I felt a kind of "death". I felt this death again after I had opened my Myofascial Release practice in Maine, and the stress of living outside of my authentic self again caused a flare in my Lyme Disease. My mental and emotional health would no longer allow me to practice. Again, my body gave out in order to provide me with an escape from a path that wasn't meant for me. With every death, you must grieve. It is an ending, and has to be processed as such. I realize as I get older that grief does not come and go easily. It never really leaves at all. It feels like it gets closer and farther away over time. And maybe that's okay. Maybe the ashes of our previous lives are what give the Phoenix it's beautiful colors as it rises. Maybe, without that grief, we would forget the lessons that we need to master before we can move on to the next chapter. Maybe grief is a part of healing.

CHAPTER 15

My childhood nickname was Smiley. Life was easy. Keep everyone happy and be good, and God will give me, and everyone I love, everlasting life in paradise. Over the years, life got more complicated, and the prize at the end faded into uncertainty. I think the goal is to be good, to be kind, to live our most authentic life, regardless of what happens. I believe it was Mother Teresa, or maybe it was just someone on Facebook, who said "Give the best you have, and it will never be enough. Give your best anyway." Maybe there isn't a weighted scale of judgment at the end of all of this. Maybe the key is just to live life in such a way that you can live with yourself.

A dear friend of mine did a Ted Talk entitled "Life isn't supposed to be good all of the time." Sadness is a part of life. It makes it even more precious when we do have moments of joy. But that's all any of us are guaranteed. Those moments. We need to appreciate them when they come to pass. We need to be okay with moments that aren't social media worthy, and realize that those times in between are just as much a reason to live as the highlight reel. Real life requires authenticity. It requires truth, humility, and self acceptance. Love is the highest vibration. It's also our "true north". We must always ask ourselves "Am I acting out of love or fear?" This isn't new information. We have heard it many times in self-help books and life improvement podcasts. It's a simple concept, but it's not simple in it's execution.

This world can go south so quickly. Any one of us can be days away from bankruptcy, sickness, complete upheaval, and even death. As much as we would like to think that we can prevent these things, we can't. It's part of being human. The trick is not to make decisions based on fear or anxiety, to try to stave these things off. The trick is to make decisions to embrace a vibrant, abundant life while we have it. Even if we are just taking this life moment by moment. There is no "good enough". I remember sitting across from my therapist and saying "I will never be enough." And she responded "For whom?" That thought still sits with me today. Am I enough for my parents? For myself? For God? Who determines what "enough" is? It's an impossible standard because really, "enough" as a concrete measure doesn't even exist. There isn't even really a right or wrong. Buddhists teach a philosophy of interdependence, this means that everything is true in relation to something else. A gray couch is dark compared to a white couch, but a gray couch is also light in comparison to a black couch. Both things are real and true. Murder might be considered a bad thing, but what about a murder performed in self defense? There is no truth, only perception based on our own life experiences. So we can't judge ourselves, and if we can't judge our own actions, then how could we possibly judge the lives or opinions of others? Maybe the purpose of life is in the ambiguity.

What I know of trauma is this. It changes us on the most fundamental level. Psychoneuroimmunology is an emerging field that teaches us that our thoughts change our physical bodies. But sometimes, that change makes us stronger. It's like when we work out, our muscles get stronger from exercise because they are being torn apart and rebuilt stronger. A tree that is constantly barraged by the wind has a stronger root system than one that has just grown pleasantly in the sunshine. Every season has a reason, and we don't always get to know what it is. That's the point of faith. I used to have an elderly patient who would get frustrated and then pause, hold her pointer and middle fingers up to her mouth, kiss them, and then "toss" the kiss up to the ceiling. I asked her why she did that and she said "I got frustrated, and realized I had to take a moment to kiss it up to God." This has nothing at all to do with religion. Even the strongest atheist of them all can "kiss it up to God" in the sense that we just need to let go of the outcome. There will always be things we can not control, and that's okay. Imagine the pressure of having to make the right decisions all of the time if everything WAS in our control. We can have the peace of knowing that even if we do everything perfectly, we might not have been able to change the outcome any more than if we made mistakes along the way. Grace is a word used mostly in the religious community. It certainly wasn't a concept taught by the Witnesses, and after I left the cult, I was enthralled not only by the idea of a God who gives Grace to his children, but also by how much more powerful it is to give Grace to ourselves. Unconditional grace.

For a while, I stalled on how to finish this book. I wanted to end with some grand equation for how to rise from the ashes and overcome trauma. I wanted to conclude the book by telling you that I was perfectly healthy in body, mind and soul. I didn't want to write a book about overcoming trauma while still feeling like an imposter that hadn't fully healed herself yet. Again, I found the answer to my worries in a conversation with my best friend. I brought up my concerns with her by saying "Well, I haven't healed all of my trauma yet, so how can I write about how I did it, if I haven't done it yet?" She said "If you are looking for a way to be done healing, you aren't in the now, and that's the only place where any healing is going to happen." This is why she's my best friend. Those words resounded in me like a gong. You heal trauma by being in the moment. You can't be healed by living anywhere else besides the present. Maybe healing isn't about reaching some zen-like state of enlightenment, where you have finally transcended all of your worries and problems. Maybe true healing is sitting with all of the scars, and bruises, and altered DNA that has come from surviving these traumas, and being okay with accepting this change as your new reality.

I learned something about Lyme disease from my dog's vet. She said the Lyme vaccine is only seventy percent effective because Lyme is able to change forms to skirt the vaccine. I thought about the fight against my own chronic Lyme as she said it. If the beast keeps changing, then the only way to coexist with it is to keep changing myself. I have to be okay with never reaching an end date. This marathon of trauma never ends. It just changes. I am able to add in new tools, but you can never go back to who you were before the trauma. That person doesn't exist anymore. And maybe that's the whole point of this earthly journey.

John Barnes, the founder of Myofascial Release says "if you think you are trying too hard, you usually are." I have found this to be a valid statement in many areas of life, not just bodywork.

Acceptance. It's a tough one. We are bombarded by social media images of these perfect lives and branding messages like "no pain, no gain." The Bible says that in order to survive we must "exert ourselves vigorously to get through the narrow door to life." We are a society that assigns worth based on productivity, degrees, and accomplishments. But what if our greatest purpose is achieved with stillness? What if just allowing ourselves to "be" is the state of our highest worth? What if we are already enough just by existing?

People always ask me how I had the strength to leave the cult and the answer is that I ran out of the strength to pretend I could stay. God made me a survivor. He gave me a fire in my belly to fight what is unjust. He gave me a husband with a Robin Hood complex, who understands my need to make things right. So many times, I have been the victim and yet, every single time I chose to trade the title of victim for the title of survivor.

When you are a foster parent, people always say "I could never do that." "I couldn't love a kid, and have to give them away." Neither can we. It's not easier for us to do it than it is for anyone else. It's the same for trauma therapists. People say "I couldn't hear the stories of all of those women suffering an abuse that horrific." We can't either. You just do it because in order for these people to have help, someone has to. People in this world need help. So much of this world is broken. The Witnesses would make you believe that we have to wait for God's Kingdom to come in order to fix it. We have to preach door to door, and tell everyone to rely on God, and then one day, once he has proved that mankind cannot rule himself, and he has allowed Satan to fuck with us sufficiently, but we still choose to worship him... then, he will turn the earth back into a paradise, and our suffering will be over. But that is a load of bull shit. The truth is that there is good and evil in every one of us. There is love and fear, right and wrong. It's at the heart of every movie and book because it resonates with all of us. We don't need to wait on God's Kingdom because God is love, and that love is already here within each one of us. We are all made in his image, the image of love. That promise of paradise is here now, it is within us every time we choose to act in accordance with love over fear. Each act of love raises the collective vibration here on Earth.

When we choose to be the "hands and feet of Christ" or act in accordance with love towards ourselves or other humans, we ARE God's promised kingdom personified. We are all capable of shifting the balance from fear to love, even if it's just for one person, for only a moment. It matters. That's all we can do. We just have to wake up, and choose to tip the scales towards love in whatever way we can. Will we end up broken? Absolutely. Will that trauma change us at the core? Undoubtedly. Do we need to do it anyway? It is the only thing that matters. Be love. Show love. Spread love. Everything else falls away. Love is the chisel on the marble. It will always set you free.

As long as there are people choosing fear over love, we can't just give up and stop helping. I have tried that over the years, many times. I quit. I give up. I withdraw and figure I need to just help myself, and my family instead of helping others. I use Mother Teresa's famous quote "help the person closest to you" as an excuse to only help my family. But then the call to do more builds within me again. We are made in

God's image so we are love, and when we do not act in accordance with our divine purpose, our bodies let us know by producing feelings of anxiety and depression. This does not mean that compassion fatigue isn't real, and that we do not need periods of time to rest and recharge so that we have something to give again. Of course we do. But, it does not mean we get to give up altogether. People who have given up, who have lost hope, are not living life to the fullest anymore. They are not experiencing the purpose of this life here on earth. So the question becomes, how do we recharge after trauma? How do we keep refueling so that we have the energy to go on "being love"? The answer to this question will be different for all of us, but it will always involve some sort of stillness, and when in doubt remember my mantra "Feel, Heal, and Grow. Surrender to the Flow."

The objective of this book is to share my story of survival. I want to explain how early in life our belief systems can change us, even on a physical level. I want people to see that Jehovah's Witnesses are a dangerous cult and not just a religion. I want to inspire people to live their truth. I want people to realize that they are both the sculptor, and the statue. I want people to know that whatever circumstance they are born into, with whatever restrictions are holding them back, it is in our power to change them. As long as we are living, we can start over again.

There is no finish line for healing. There is only growth. Obstacles, and overcoming those obstacles, are what cause our soul to grow. Life is a long time. In this life I have been a religious fanatic, I have been pro life, and the mother of a son. I was sure that this world was about to end. I was thin. As I played all of these roles, I was so confident in these beliefs that

I would have died to protect them. None of these roles are mine anymore. Now I am a mother of two daughters, a wife to Jimmy, socially liberal, and fiscally conservative. I am a Health At Every Size activist, pro-choice, a writer, and a proud member of the LGBTQ community. I also realize that although parts of me are how God made me to be, and will not change, at the same time, I am allowed to change my mind. Every day that I am alive is a day that I can choose to learn and grow, and it is okay if learning something new changes my perspective. That's sort of the point of being alive. It doesn't make me a hypocrite, or any less worthy of feeling passionately about the beliefs while I have them. It does, however, make me feel more grace and openness to people who feel or believe differently than I do, because I was once on their side of the fence as well. I realize that it is not the belief that sets us apart, but our judgment of someone else for experiencing the world differently than we do. I wouldn't say that I am a Buddhist, but I do love the Buddhist philosophy of impermanence. In Buddhism, impermanence means that everything is always changing, from our emotions, and surroundings, to the cells of our body. We have to be willing to accept that nothing stays the same. The only truth is love. It is the only constant. Everything else can come and go around it.

I choose to continue to rise. In the end, all I can do is encourage you to find your truth, and use it as a compass for your life. Just living a life outside of our authentic selves is a traumatic experience. We also have to remember that who we are changes, and we have permission to change our lives to reflect that growth, as many times as we need to, in order to continue to mirror our most authentic self. We are meant to grow and change, and our perspective is meant to shift as well. There is no black and white, no right or wrong, only different perspectives. When we cling to one "truth" with so much energy that our "rightness" overcomes the vibration of love, then that "truth" becomes dangerous.

It was only in recent years that I decided to read the book *A Wrinkle in Time* by Madeleine L'Engle. When I was in middle school, we were supposed to discuss it in class, but my mother forbade me to read it. She went to the principal, and said that it was inappropriate for me to read as a true Christian, so that poor man had to make me read something else entirely. As an adult, I decided I wanted to see what it was all about. I was completely enthralled with the book. Its message that courage and love together can overcome any obstacle is the message that has brought me the most peace in my life. Over and over again, courage and love have solved every problem I have ever had.

Writing this book feels a lot like running naked through the streets and shouting out my biggest insecurities for others to hear, but it also feels like the most courageous thing I have ever done, and it is one hundred percent rooted in love. I hope that this book will encourage people to continue to question their truths. I hope it will remind everyone who reads it to give endless grace to themselves and to others, and to love with reckless abandon. It is only in choosing courageous acts of love that we raise our own vibration, and the vibration of all of those we come in contact with. That increase in vibration is what healing is all about. It isn't a target to be reached, it has no finish line, and it can not be wrapped up in a perfect package. It is messy, and ever changing. It is the human experience. We are given this life, this journey, as a mirror of our soul's condition. We get to choose what to do with the reflection that looks back at us.

THE END